THE MYSTERY OF THE CHURCH

THE MYSTERY OF THE CHURCH

Studies by

YVES CONGAR

Translated by

A. V. Littledale

HELICON PRESS
BALTIMORE 1960

This book was originally published in French as two separate books: *Esquisses du mystère de l'Église* and *La Pentecôte: Chartres, 1956* by Les Editions du Cerf, Paris.

Nihil obstat: Carolus Davis, S.T.L.
Censor deputatus

Imprimatur: E. Morrogh Bernard
Vic. gen.

Westmonasterii, die 31a Octobris, 1959

The *Nihil obstat* and *Imprimatur* are a declaration that a book or pamphlet is considered to be free from doctrinal or moral error. It is not implied that those who have granted the *Nihil obstat* and *Imprimatur* agree with the contents, opinions or statements expressed.

Library of Congress Catalog Card Number: 60-7793

Made and printed in Great Britain by WOOD WESTWORTH & CO. LTD., for the publisher, HELICON PRESS, INC., 5305 East Drive, Baltimore 27, Maryland, in November 1959

Contents

Translator's Note

The present volume comprises two works of Père Congar on the subject of the Church. The first is entitled *La Pentecôte Chartres*, published in 1956, and reproduced here under the heading, *The Church and Pentecost*. The other is his *Esquisses du Mystère de l'Eglise*, the new edition of 1953.

It is obviously appropriate to join them in one volume by reason of their subject-matter, though the style and tone of the two are very different. The smaller work purports to be a discourse delivered to a group of pilgrims as they made their dusty way towards Chartres, where they were due to arrive for the feast of Pentecost. The manner, therefore, is naturally colloquial, even breezy; we see, in our mind's eye, the shorts and the loaded haversacks, which, to judge from some of the references, must have held, besides articles of more common necessity, at least some of the volumes of Migne.

The other studies are, of course, more academic in manner. The preface, which is here placed at the beginning of the whole volume, was written for the *Esquisses*; it has been adapted by altering the enumeration of the studies it refers to. On the other hand, it seemed better to place the passages from Swete and Möhler, printed as an appendix to *La Pentecôte*, at the end of the first study, to which they refer.

Preface

The second of the studies in this volume was written in May 1937; it was intended to form part of a work by various Catholic authors written for those attending the great ecumenical Conferences and, in particular, the second Conference on practical Christianity, which met at Oxford in July of that year. This work, edited by M. O. Iserland, has appeared only in its German version (*Die Kirche Christi*, Benziger, 1941). Our intention in reproducing this study is to present, mainly for Christians separated from us, a comprehensive view of the mystery of the Church, in which the different elements of the mystery are justly proportioned, those which are derivative or secondary being set forth in the light of the primary and principal ones from which they proceed. At the same time, we have tried to keep as close as possible to the revealed sources on which all theology of the Church must depend. Thus we have attended not so much to the development as to the interconnection and exactness of the ideas put forward.

The third essay, written in February 1939, is a paper read to the London Aquinas Society. It aims at bringing out the characteristic features of the theological structure of the mystery of the Church as conceived by St. Thomas Aquinas, and at observing the economy of this structure, the connection or articulation of its elements. It is a synthesis, rather than an exposition, of the Thomist theology *De Ecclesia*.

The same may be said of the fourth essay, an article published in *La Vie Spirituelle* (1937), whose aim is to acquaint the faithful with the essential elements of the mystery of the mystical body as a fact of the spiritual order. It is somewhat brief, and we hope to treat it more fully some other time; its general idea, however, we hold to be extremely fruitful, namely that the substance of the mystical body is living faith.

In a general presentation of the Thomist conception of the Church, it is impossible to go into very close detail. Certain important aspects inadequately treated in the present study have been well brought out in two studies which appeared later. Durquennes in *La définition de l' Eglise d'après saint Thomas d'Aquin* (Louvain, 1943) has some valuable things to say about the terminology used by St. Thomas in defining the Church and about his conception of its juridical structure. The most notable outcome of his work is the similarity he establishes between the definition of the Church as *congregatio* (*collectio*) *fidelium* and the notion of corporation current in the time of St. Thomas. Many of the ideas put forward in our own work could, as a result of these studies, either be put in a stronger light (as, for instance, what we have said about the unity of the Church through faith and the theological virtues) or else completed (the Church as a social body; the analysis of its organization and of its external means of realization).

In addition, the Abbé Vautier has published a methodical analysis of the various passages in which St. Thomas treats of the Holy Spirit as the source of the unity of the Church. He shows how St. Thomas has had from the very beginning, and kept to the end, though he never returned to it, a lively and original perception of the fact that the ultimate principle of the unity of the Church is the Holy Spirit, not only through his motion on account of which all is distributed and accomplished in the Church, but particularly on account of his indwelling, unique as he is and ever the same, in all the just. M. Vautier goes further and says that, according to St. Thomas, the Holy Spirit is (materially) the object, individually unique and the same, of the faith and charity of all the faithful. Thus the idea of unity we have put forward needs to be completed: to the unity of motion of the

Holy Spirit must be added, over and above the specific unity of all the faithful in faith, hope and charity, a twofold numerical unity, that of a single object of knowledge and love and, more especially, that of one and the same divine guest dwelling in the souls of the just.

We are glad to have our attention called to passages we were already familiar with and which we may have been at fault in not making more use of in our own lecture. Moreover, since the articles of M. Vautier, there has appeared the second volume of Journet's monumental treatise, *The Church of the Word Incarnate*. The theology of what the author constantly calls the created soul of the Church, that is to say of charity "as sacramental and orientated" or strictly "ecclesial", is, with great profundity, breadth and precision, set in relation with that of the uncreated soul of the Church, the Holy Spirit. The theology of this work, though its terminology is, like that of M. Vautier, open to certain objections, is evidently an application of St. Thomas's own synthesis and of the ideas to which M. Vautier has directed attention. We recommend the reader to turn to this remarkable and voluminous work if he wishes to understand in its full depth what we have only been able to touch upon in a short lecture.

* * *

These studies of a doctrinal nature, in which the mystery of the Church is, on the whole, considered in its essence, are followed by one whose scope is somewhat different. It was written in January 1937 and published in the *Bulletin des Missions* of September 1938, and may seem to concern not so much the essence of the mystery of the Church as a merely peripheral aspect of its life. Yet the more we reflect on the matter, the more important appears the idea brought out and vindicated in this study. It happens often enough that Protestants in the name of the Bible, and Anglicans in the name of history, object to us on the ground of the difference between the Church as it has actually become with us and even the Church whose theory we set forth, and the Church as it seems to have been in its origins, in the Gospel, or at this or that period in the past. To take, for example, the Papacy. How can we justify its actual development—for which Catholics claim that it is not a purely human excrescence, outside the essence of the Church—when we consider the Gospel texts, certain facts of the early history of the Church, certain early documents or the absence of written evidence, and, finally, the general absence, in the earliest times, of an explicit consciousness that the Papacy formed part of the Church? Why, for example, when Justin and Origen, each in his age, wrote a summary of the Christian faith, did they make no allusion to the primacy of the Roman See? Why, if the text, *Tu es Petrus,* means what we say it does, was the Church unaware of its significance for at least two centuries?

This is a serious difficulty, one which is at the root of a number of other difficulties which raise an insurmountable barrier between Protestants or Anglicans and ourselves. No doubt, each separate difficulty can be met in scholarly fashion; our text-books of apologetics and dictionaries are full of arguments about texts and facts, and are adept at reconciling objections. But the real difficulty is of a general nature; it has to do, fundamentally, with the Church's essence, and calls for a comprehensive answer on this basis. It is necessary to justify the contention, by appealing to the very nature of things, that the reality which is the Church transcends the consciousness men have of it, the expressions they use about it, even those used by the inspired authors; that things not to be found in the texts are truly part of the Church's essence, or rather that they were not at first perceived in the texts. It has to be shown that it is not so much the text that explains the Church's reality as the reality that explains and makes clear the text; that, in this way, the life of the Church completes our entry into the revelation of its mystery; that the Church is to be fully understood only by being seen from within, and, ultimately, only by those who live within it.

Can we not, from this point of view, give a meaning which is not only acceptable, but profoundly Catholic and really necessary, to certain contentions which, though ill-stated and misapplied by modernist or near-modernist authors, yet contain at least some part of indisputable truth? We allude to the tendency to take into consideration, along with the inspired and authoritative sources of Christian thought, the actual reality of the Church, the facts of the Christian life and the experience which, on the side of the faithful themselves, corresponds to the acts of divine Providence. Cannot, we repeat, the idea be taken in an acceptable and profoundly Catholic sense that divine Revelation, objectively definitive and concluded, comes to be developed subjectively, that is to be "realized" and perceived within the Church itself, "*re credita eveniente*", in the words of Albert the Great; that, in this way, the Church, far from having to turn its gaze exclusively to the past and to the documents of the past, is also open to the present and the future, constantly developing without the least loss of continuity or of its unity through the ages? Surely this standpoint gives us a more genuine, richer, more "traditional" idea of Tradition, an idea of Tradition considered as something living and active, the consciousness which the Church, without foregoing any of its past, takes progressively and possesses now of its own content. Recent studies of very great interest (Guitton, Dufour) show how a Tradition of this kind arose in the time of the apostles and how, among other things, it explains the deeper understanding of the Gospel facts reached between the first writers and St. John. The latter, when he says, in regard to Christ's words about the destruction of the temple, that the disciples remembered them and understood them after his resurrection (John ii. 22), gives us the first example of what we here suggest. Revelation had been given, but the Church came to an understanding of its pronouncements only in the light of the event and through the action of the Holy Spirit, the source of Tradition, which is, at one and the same time, conservation and progress. This implies no evolutionism, no relativism through an undue recourse to "life"; it is simply the recognition and explanation of a fact.

The longer we reflect on these matters, the more we realize how true and profound they are, how they involve a whole conception of the mystery of the Church, of the conditions of life in the Church and of the understanding of its mystery. The Church is not an artificial construction which is made, or should be made, by harking back to texts prior and external to it. This is the conception implied in all the Protestant or reformed standpoints. On the contrary, the Church is a living organism, animated and governed by the Holy Spirit, one which contains, vitally, its law within itself. It cannot be understood from the outside, solely by way of scientific inquiry or criticism. Historical and rational vindications are not lacking, but they are never adequate to the reality; this, in fact, is grasped only by the Church itself and by each individual in the degree in which he lives in it, in its communion.

I

The Church and Pentecost

"THE FIRST BOOK which I wrote, Theophilus, was concerned with all that Jesus set out to do and teach, until the day came when he was taken up into heaven. He then laid a charge, by the power of the Holy Spirit, on the apostles whom he had chosen. He had shown them, by many proofs, that he was still alive, after his passion; throughout the course of forty days he had been appearing to them, and telling them about the kingdom of God; and now he gave them orders, as he shared a meal with them, not to leave Jerusalem, but to wait there for the fulfilment of the Father's promise. You have heard it, he said, from my own lips; John's baptism, I told you, was with water, but there is a baptism with the Holy Spirit which you are to receive, not many days from this.

"And his companions asked him, Lord, dost thou mean to restore the dominion to Israel here and now? But he told them: It is not for you to know the times and seasons which the Father has fixed by his own authority. Enough for you, that the Holy Spirit will come upon you, and you will receive strength from him; you are to be my witnesses in Jerusalem and throughout Judaea, in Samaria, yes, and to the ends of the earth. When he had said this, they saw him lifted up, and a cloud caught him away from their sight. And as they strained their eyes towards heaven, to watch his journey, all at once two men in white garments were standing at their side. Men of Galilee, they said, why do you stand here looking heavenwards? He who has been taken from you into heaven, this same Jesus, will come back in the same fashion, just as you have watched him going into heaven. Then, from the mountain which is called Olivet, they went back to Jerusalem; the distance from Jerusalem is not great, a sabbath day's journey. Coming in, they went up into the upper room where they dwelt, Peter and John, James and Andrew, Philip and Thomas, Bartholomew and Matthew, James the son of Alphaeus and Simon the Zealot, and Judas the brother of James. All these, with one mind, gave themselves to prayer, together with Mary the mother of Jesus, and the rest of the women and his brethren. . . .

"When the day of Pentecost came round, while they were all gathered together in unity of purpose, all at once a sound came from heaven like that of a strong wind blowing, and filled the whole house where they were sitting. Then appeared to them what seemed to be tongues of fire, which parted and came to rest on each of them; and they were all filled with the Holy Spirit, and began to speak in strange languages, as the Spirit gave utterance to each. Among those who were dwelling in Jerusalem at this time were devout Jews from every country under heaven; so, when the noise of this went abroad, the crowd which gathered was in bewilderment; each man severally heard them speak in his own language. And they were all beside themselves with astonishment. Are they not all Galileans speaking? they asked. How is it that each of us hears them talking his own native tongue? There are Parthians among us and Medes and Elamites; our homes are in Mesopotamia or Judaea or Cappadocia; in Pontus or Asia, Phrygia or Pamphylia, Egypt or the parts of Libya round Cyrene; some of us are visitors from Rome, some of us are Jews and other proselytes; there are Cretans among us, too, and Arabians; and each has been hearing them tell of God's wonders in his own language. So they were all beside themselves with perplexity, and asked one another, What can this mean? There were others who said, mockingly, They have had their fill of new wine.

"But Peter, with the eleven apostles at his side, stood there and raised his voice to speak to them: Men of Judaea, he said, and all you who are dwelling in Jerusalem, I must tell you this; listen to what I have to say. These men are not drunk, as you suppose; it is only the third hour of the day. This is what was foretold by the prophet Joel: In the last times, God says, I will pour out my spirit upon all mankind, and your sons and daughters will be prophets. Your young men shall see visions, and your old men shall dream dreams; and I will pour out my spirit in those days upon my servants and handmaids, so that they will prophesy" (Acts i. 1–14; ii. 1–18).

* * *

This year we go to Chartres at the time of Pentecost, and the subject we have to meditate on is precisely this fact of Pentecost, which the Church celebrates today.

Pentecost is not just an "ideological" feast, designed to bring out a particular dogma, as is the feast of the Trinity or Corpus Christi. Nor is its purpose to celebrate the Person of the Holy Spirit; there is, in fact, no special feast of the Holy Spirit, any more than there is one of the Father or the Word. What it is, occurring, as it does, between spring and summer, is an annual commemoration of *the fact* of the coming of the Holy Spirit on and into the Church (cf. Leo XIII's encyclical, *Divinum illud munus*, of the 9th of May 1897). Pentecost, as part of the Proper of the Season in the liturgical year, is the celebration of a mystery of our salvation, as is Christmas or Easter.

What exactly do we mean by a mystery of salvation? It means one of those decisive acts or moments selected by God's grace, an event which, once it has come to pass, has set up for ever a new principle or element in the existing relation between man and God. For that reason, the celebration of mysteries like Christmas, Easter or Pentecost is not a simple commemoration in a purely intellectual sense, a simple recalling to mind. In celebrating one of these, I put myself in the flowing stream of God's gift, a gift ever working to effect in time what he initiated on a particular day. My God is not inactive, but living; the Apocalypse, echoing Exodus iii. 14, calls him, as if by his own name, "He who is, and ever was, and is still to come" (Apoc. i. 4; iv. 8). What is said of him may be said of his acts, may be said of Pentecost; it was, it is, and it is still to come. And since, this year, we have the happiness of thinking and speaking of it, *while actually celebrating it*, we will try to make these chapters and our meditations, not merely alternate with our prayer, but intertwine with it, to enter ourselves into the mystery and let it enter us; we will bring to our celebration of it an effort of mind, of muscle, our whole attention, and it, in turn, will nourish our life by what it brings of strength, faith and love.

The love it will stir up in us, is, specifically, fraternal. Indeed, this love must be always present; it is the very law of Christian living. But it belongs particularly to Pentecost, and is one of the specific conditions of a true celebration of the feast. On that day, the Holy Spirit was given to *each one*, but he was, too, given to the disciples *gathered together*, and gathered in oneness of mind, That is what is expressed in the *Acts* by the constant use of the formula *epi to auto*, "all together" (i. 15; ii. 1, 44, 47). There is a remarkable passage of Moehler to this effect, which is to be found at the end of this chapter. So then what forms the spiritual climate of our Pentecost is not only our combined prayer and meditation, but the fraternal concord of our journey, with all the occasions it involves of service, concern and common consent.

We agree, then, on this: in our pilgrimage to Chartres to celebrate the fact of Pentecost, unique yet ever active, our subject of meditation is this fact itself. It is not the Person of the Holy Spirit in himself or a theology of the Holy Spirit we are concerned with, not even, strictly speaking, a theology of his gifts or of his life in us, though, of necessity, we shall touch upon that, but the *fact* of Pentecost and all that it means for ever for the faith and life of the Church.

PENTECOST, THE FIFTIETH DAY OF THE PASCH

This is what it means, etymologically. The word, in Latin and modern Western languages, is but the transposition of a Greek word meaning fiftieth. Its use derives from a corresponding word in the Jewish liturgy, and that, too, is of great interest and importance for an understanding of the Christian meaning. So, then, Pentecost is (but) the 50th day of a unique feast, that of Easter.

Easter—that conveys something to us. One of the great rediscoveries of the last ten years is that of the Pascal mystery as the centre of all the life of Christianity. That is, perhaps, the finest result of post-war Biblical and liturgical research. We have discovered anew—not only by the mind, but by a living celebration which is itself vivifying—that the whole Christian life has its centre and origin in Christ's "passage", through death in the flesh, to a life according to the Spirit. "The death he died was a death, once for all, to sin; the life he now lives is a life that looks towards God" (Rom. vi. 10; the whole passage should be read). We know that Easter is not only the anniversary of Christ's resurrection, but embraces the whole mystery of the new life he gained for us by his "passage", his death-resurrection-ascension all together. Consider the *Unde et memores,* which follows the consecration at Mass, and books like Bouyer's *The Pascal Mystery* and Daniélou's *Bible et liturgie.*

What Christ is and has done, he is and has done *for us,* for our benefit. Once we have grasped this, we are at the centre of the great Christian reality. See, for example, what Durrwell says on St. Paul (*La Résurrection de Jésus, mystère de salut*), Mersch on the Fathers of the Church (*Le Corps mystique du Christ, Etude historique,* 2 vols.), and Grossouw on St. John (*Revelation and Redemption,* Geoffrey Chapman, 1958). Their insight, so direct, simple and full, into the Christian mystery comes from their grasp of this fundamental truth, that the mystery of Jesus is not confined to what he was in himself, but includes us as well. All that we find in the Gospels and the writings of the apostles cries out that

God's purposes and his gifts do not stop short at the incarnation, but embrace the whole Church in their scope—Christ is the stock of the whole plan which is the vine; he is the head of the body; he is, for mankind, a second Adam, a second origin of a race that is renewed, and so on.

In short, *there is a dynamism coming from God for men through Christ.*

It is not the only dynamism at work in the world. Look around for a moment and see the great movements which are the stuff of history, and consider what sets them off, the dynamism impelling them.

Nature's renewal in Spring, all the pulsing of sap and the luxuriance of fresh foliage along our roads to Chartres—whence its dynamism?

What is it that drives man to woman, the child to its mother and the young mother to her child?

The impulse to discover, the thirst for knowledge—where lies its dynamism?

The great movements of history, migrations, invasions, the great conquests. Alexander, Islam, Napoleon. What is the dyanamism? The movement of the workers; Communism, and all the rest.

Now, among the great things of the world, the great movements of history, there is, whether we are part of it or not, that of Christianity, the Church. There is the faith. If it is a question of positive faith in Revelation, in the Word, it began at a point of that particular time in which Christ occupies, relatively to us, roughly the middle, and of which he is for evermore the centre. If it is a question of the Gospel, of that great apostolic movement embracing the world, which is the Church, what is its dynamism, when did it first start? What is the source which brings to pass, in men, that holiness which was our subject of meditation last year in that atmosphere of fairyland brought to life, of a great dream come true, which was for me, with you, that of Chartres?

The answer give by Revelation is: The Holy Spirit, since the time of Christ. It is the Spirit of Jesus Christ.

The moving force, the animating principle, of everything Christian, everything holy, since Christ, is the Holy Spirit. He it is who leads us back to the God of holiness, and unites us to him.

1. *Jesus Christ, by his death and resurrection, merited for us the gift of the Spirit. Pentecost is the fruit of the Pasch.*

There is one point, one moment, at which this movement began. The point is the pierced side of Christ on the cross. The moment is that of the outpouring of the Holy Spirit, which followed on the Pasch (the death-resurrection-ascension) of Christ.

Here let us remind ourselves of a few passages which show this conclusively.

Luke xxiv. 25–26: "Was it not to be expected that the Christ should undergo these sufferings, and enter so into his glory?" John vii. 33–39: "On the last and greatest day of the feast, Jesus stood there and cried aloud, 'If any man is thirsty, let him come to me and drink; yes, if a man believes in me, as the scripture says, Fountains of living water shall flow from his bosom.' He was speaking here of the Spirit, which was to be received by those who learned to believe in him; the Spirit which had not yet been given to men, because Jesus had not been raised to glory". John xvii. 1–2: "Father, the time has come; give glory now to thy Son, that thy Son may give the glory to thee. Thou hast put him in authority over all mankind, to bring eternal life to all those thou hast entrusted to him". John xix, 28, 30: "And now Jesus knew well that all was achieved . . . Jesus drank the vinegar and said, 'It is achieved'. Then he bowed his head and yielded up his spirit". John xix. 33–34: "When they came to Jesus, and found him already dead, they did not break his legs, but one of the soldiers opened his side with a spear; and immediately blood and water flowed out".

St. John places the mystery with which we are here concerned in the category of *glory*, and this certainly appears a little puzzling.

But let us make an effort to enter into his thought. It forms a wonderfully harmonious and integrated structure. Dominating the whole is the great theology of the Prologue—all comes from the Father, the Principle who has no principle, from whom the Son holds all that he is, to whom he refers all he has received: "We had sight of his glory, glory such as belongs to the Father's only-begotten Son, full of grace and truth" (i. 14). Christ's glory is precisely that which an only Son *holds from his Father*; it *consists* of receiving from the Father, of obeying him, of doing everything in dependence on him, of referring all to him. Read, from this standpoint, John iii. 34–35; v. 17–20; v. 30; vi. 57; vii. 16. There we have the conception of glory held by St. John and the Gospel; whereas, in the pagan or merely human view, glory consists in possessing personal distinction from the good opinion and praise of one's fellow-men—it is, so to speak, horizontal. (Cp. Pascal, *Pensées*, 150–153, 318, 323, 324, 401, 404.) But for Christ and according to the Gospel, it consists in nullifying oneself in seeking the glory and will *of the Father*—it is, so to speak, vertical. See John vii. 18; viii. 54; v. 54, and compare the famous passage of St. Paul to the Philippians, ii. 7, sq.: Christ's glory consists in obeying the will and plan of God even to the death of the cross, that is why God exalts him and gives him a name above every name, the name and title of Lord. That is the reason why Christ's Passion is the decisive moment of his glorification, and it explains certain passages which may appear strange, John x. 17–18; viii. 28; xii. 23–24, 27–28; xiii. 31–32, and those cited above, John xvii. 1, etc.

My fellow-pilgrim, if you want to understand fully the mystery of Christ and of the life you are called to in Christ, read these texts, meditate on them; stop an hour—is that too much to ask?—in the course of your crowded, turbulent life, to know at last yourself and your God.

This is his plan, in which we have to place ourselves by faith. By glorifying the Father through obedience unto death and the death of the cross—"Father, if it be possible, let this chalice pass from me; yet, not my will, but thine, be done"—the Son finds his glory *as Son,* and he, in turn, is glorified by the Father, in us; the grain, by dying, brings forth much fruit; his death, so far from being an end, is a beginning. The Church has its beginning in Christ's "Consummatum est", which means, not only, my life is over, but, I have fulfilled all thy will. From his side opened by the lance flows the living water that is the image of the Spirit, as is to be seen from so many other passages (John iv. 10–14; vii. 37-39; Apoc. vii. 17; xxii. 17). Christian symbolism and the liturgy are full of this.

You have, of course, seen, in many churches, a large crucifix hanging at the entrance to the sanctuary. The sanctuary represents the life of grace, the life of heaven, and the cross is the way of approach to it. Perhaps, too, you have seen, in the earlier editions of Lubac's *Catholicisme,* the pictures juxtaposed of the carrying of the cross from Rheims Cathedral and of the Pentecost of Vézelay, with the inscription, "That was the condition of this." You have noticed that the first lesson in the liturgy of the vigil of Pentecost is the sacrifice of Isaac, the type of Christ's sacrifice, showing that obedience to death is the condition of living for God and the prelude to resurrection. Or else, with your knowledge of the Fathers and the theologians of old, you have come across some of those numerous passages showing the Church, under the symbol of water and blood—the sacraments—issuing from the open side of Christ on the cross, as Eve, the mother of the living, came out from the side of Adam in his sleep—an idea taken up again in the encyclical *Mystici corporis.* All this serves as an illustration of what Christ proclaimed when he cried aloud in the temple on that most solemn of feasts, the feast of Tabernacles (the end of September): "Fountains of living water shall flow from his bosom [that of the Messias]". He was speaking here of the Spirit. (John vii. 38–39).

In short, if it is the Holy Spirit whose action brings into being the Church, and causes salvation and holiness wherever it is found, his dynamism passes through a particular point and moment, namely, Christ in his Pasch, by which he glorifies his Father. For us, everything flows from that.

See now how Pentecost is but the 50th day of the feast of the Pasch. It came about "when the fifty days [the pascal period] was accomplished" (Acts ii. 1). The fiftieth day, that is to say the fullness, according to a symbolism based on the laws of ancient symbolism; (so important for an understanding of the real meaning of things) for $7 \times 7 + 1$ (=superplenitude)$=50$. Pentecost, then, is the fulness of the Pasch. So it is that St. Augustine says, in one of his sermons, at the beginning of the 5th century: "See how the solemnity of the Pasch has reached its conclusion without losing any of its splendour. The Pasch was the beginning of grace, Pentecost the crown" (*Sermo* 43: P.L., vol. 28, col. 1235 sq.). For the liturgy and the Fathers, the period following Easter, though taking up fifty days of the calendar, was yet only one and the same feast, which St. Athanasius calls "the great Sunday" (see Daniélou, *Bible et liturgie*, p. 429 sq.).

From this point of view, the fact that fifty days had elapsed since the Pasch is of no great importance. It is, indeed, interesting in other respects, and we shall see later what significance lies in the coincidence of the sudden outpouring of the Holy Spirit with the Jewish celebration of Pentecost. But as regards the christological meaning of Pentecost, which is primary, it is of little consequence. If we had no *Acts* to give us exact chronological details (i. 3; ii. 1), we might easily conclude from St. Luke's Gospel (xxiv) that the Ascension took place the very next day after the Pasch, or even, were we reduced, if we may so speak, to the Gospel of St. John, on the very evening of the Pasch (cf. John xx. 19–23). For St. John, the important thing was to stress the connection between the gift of the Spirit and the "historical Christ", or, more precisely still, between the gift of the Spirit and the Passion (cf. the above quotations from John vii. 38–39; xix. 30, 33–34).

We are left with this simple and very important fact of the essential bond between Pentecost and the Pasch. Pentecost is simply the Pasch taken as completed, with its fruit, the Spirit. Jesus died, rose, and went up to heaven—that is his Pasch—only to communicate to us the Spirit. That is why the ancient sacramentaries, the Leonine, Gelasian, Gregorian, from which comes the text of the Masses in our Missal, have the following prayer: "Almighty and eternal God, who didst will to include in this mysterious Pentecost the whole of our Pasch. . . ." Again, it is why, just as Easter is called the "feast of feasts", St. John Chrysostom calls Pentecost "the metropolis, the capital of the feasts" (*Hom. II de Pentec.*: P.G., vol. 50, col. 463). The feast of feasts, greatest of feasts—not only because the carpets are brought out, all the candlesticks are ablaze, there is a greater abundance of flowers and more noise from the organ; but because it is, in a sense, the ONE feast, that which gives all others their character of feast. Pilgrim to Chartres, we shall sing with all our heart, we shall have a splendid and glorious celebration—not to excite the beholders or ourselves, but because our heart will be so full and the Holy Spirit will stir us so strongly from the heart to the lips that we shall have no choice but to sing. Because we are going to celebrate on the way and in THE cathedral the feast of feasts, the fulness of the Pasch which makes us free, in Christ, for the service of God and of every man in God.

2. *The functions of Christ and the Holy Spirit, respectively*

If you have followed me to this point, you have now to make a fresh effort; for we have to make quite clear what is the function of the Holy Spirit in relation to Christ. Here we enter upon a theology of the Holy Spirit in himself. The task is absolutely necessary and, though perhaps arduous, well worth while.

God's plan in our regard, as made known by Revelation—what, following the Fathers, we might call the "Economy" (of salvation) follows, so to speak, the structure of God himself. It is fundamentally the plan of the Creed, which is Trinitarian, and which follows at one and the same time the order of the "procession" of the divine Persons and the order of God's work, for the three great decisive moments of this are appropriated to these Persons. The three of which we speak are the creation, the redemption, and the work of sanctification or the communication of the divine life. Revelation shows us God committing himself more and more deeply to his creation, giving himself more and more, to the point of admitting man to a participation in his life. It is one single work of God's and, from the outset, its aim was to draw man into communion with him, a communion which begins with the Father, the Principle who has no other—whose special characteristic is to be the love which gives, *Agape* (cf. Rom. v. 5 and 2; Cor. xiii. 13), which is realised by the Son who is sent by the Father, and consummated by the Holy Spirit who is sent by the Father and the Son. The Father creates by love; and it is true that therein the Son and the Holy Spirit are also at work with him; the three Persons cannot be separated. But when a revelation and salvation are to be brought to men, it is the Son who is sent and, thereby, committed personally. Then, when the Son's revelation and salvation (or grace) are to be established in the hearts of men and taken into them, it is the Holy Spirit who is sent and, thereby, committed personally to the work of God in its consummation.

In this connection, we may make use of the following images, the first of which, at any rate, is a traditional one. The Father may be considered as the arm (the power from which the movement arises), the Son as the hand, the Holy Spirit as the fingers forming in us the image of God (Notice that the comparison of the Holy Spirit with the finger of God, which comes into Christian iconography and the *Veni Creator* is supported by Luke xi. 20 read in conjunction with Matthew xii. 28). Or again, the Father is the root, the Son the stem or the vine, the Holy Spirit the fruit. In fact, we speak of the "fruits of the Spirit" (Gal. v. 21 sq.); he is the term of the movement of giving, the final and sweet-tasting product of the movement of life imparted to us.

These are all material images, and they are useful to express the continuity of the movement of giving and the homogeneity (in the theological term, the consubstantiality—the same nature or substance) of the divine Persons. But they are inadequate to convey the character of true Persons which belongs to the Father, the Son and the Spirit. Further, it is not too difficult for us to conceive of the Father and the Son as Persons; for, on the one hand, there is the Incarnation, where we know that the Person of Christ is the Son or the Word of God; on the other, we are helped in our effort to envisage and express this mystery by the analogy of the father-son relation as it exists on the human plane. But we have nothing corresponding with these when we come to the Holy Spirit. Besides, there are even passages in Scripture which could tell in favour of an idea which was inexact or inadequate, those in which the Holy Spirit seems to be presented as without a real and fully personal character, but as simply an impersonal force, by which God acts in this world. At times, too, it would seem as if the Spirit is identified with the glorified Christ, with the "Lord" who is, as it were, constituted by it (1 Cor. xv. 45; Cor. iii. 17). What is more, we see continually, in St. Paul in particular, but in St. John, too, that the Holy Spirit and Christ *do the same thing*; constantly what is attributed to Christ's action is also attributed to the Holy Spirit (see, for instance, Rom. viii. 9 sq.). Prat and Deissmann have drawn up a whole list of these correlated and parallel statements. In St. John, the Holy Spirit, called by Christ "another Paraclete", effects that return of Christ to his followers so often spoken of in passages of the Gospel used in the liturgy of the time between the Ascension and Pentecost (cf. John xiv. 18; xvi. 22–25). The letters contained in the second and third chapters of the Apocalypse are presented both as coming *from Christ* and as "what the Spirit says to the Churches".

As is often the case, the very difficulty points to the solution and leads to a deeper understanding of the relation of the Holy Spirit to Christ.

First of all, the New Testament frequently implies that the Spirit possesses a real and fully personal character. Christ speaks of him as "another Paraclete", personal like himself (John xiv.

16–17). St. Paul, like St. John, shows him as the object of a second mission, after that of the Son and of the same kind (Gal. iv. 4–6), and speaks of him as of a real Subject of acts, assisting us, praying and interceding (Rom. viii. 15, 26, 27); very often, too, the spirit is mentioned in a Trinitarian formula, parallel with and perfectly equal to the Father and the Son. All this can be found in developed form in any theological work or dictionary, and particularly in Prat's *Theology of St. Paul* and Lebreton's *Origines du dogme de la Trinité*.

The Holy Spirit, then, is a Person, just as the Word is. He is not just the energy by which the glorified Christ acts in us. His mission is a distinct one and proper to him. But "he does not speak of himself", he says only what he has heard (John xvi. 13); his action in the Church is to bring to mind what Christ said (xiv. 26). Thus, Christ revealed the mystery of God and proclaimed the Gospel; the Holy Spirit makes his message ever present and keeps it living.

Likewise, Christ established the apostolic mission but the Holy Spirit makes this mission actual and works together with the Apostolate to make it fruitful and to assure the validity of the hierarchical functions. These aspects of his work will be treated later.

Again, the Spirit makes the sacraments effective, but they are administered in the name of Christ (1 Cor. vi. 11). Christ instituted the sacraments, but the Spirit gives them their power of sanctifying us; and so his coming is prayed for in Baptism, Holy Orders, the Eucharist.

In short, if, as regards us, the Spirit is creative ("Veni Creator Spiritus"), he is simply completing what was established by Christ. The reality would seem to be that there is one single work but it has two moments, of which the first is appropriated to the Incarnate Word, the second to the Holy Spirit. In the first, the form of salvation is set down or realized; in the second, life is infused into it, the form receives movement and produces its living fruit.

This would seem to be a kind of law of God's action. First of all, he formed Adam, *then* he breathed into him the breath of life (Gen. ii. 7). In the great vision of Ezechiel (xxxvii), the bones come together, skeletons are formed and are covered with flesh, and *then* the spirit comes into them and they become (again) living. (See also Isaias xlii. 5). Likewise, God delivered his people from Egypt, *then* he sanctified them by the covenant and his dwelling among them; so, too, Christ redeemed us and established his mystical body, *then* he communicated to it life through his Spirit.

As to the Church, Christ constituted it in being in the time of his life on earth, instituting the office of apostle, the sacraments, the primacy of Peter; then, by sending the Holy Spirit at Pentecost, he gave it the breath of life. Or, if we speak of the Temple of God, Christ it was who built it (Eph. ii. 22), and the Holy Spirit dwells in it (1 Cor. iii. 16–17). What about our condition as adopted sons of God? It was Christ who, by his Incarnation, acquired the right for us, but the Holy Spirit brings it about and causes us to act in a corresponding way. The way in which St. Paul speak on this point is highly significant. "God", he says, "sent out his Son on a mission to us. He took birth from a woman, took birth as a subject of the law, so as to ransom those who were subject to the law, and make us sons by adoption" (Gal. iv. 4–5); "To prove that you are sons, God has sent out the Spirit of his Son *into our hearts*, crying out in us, Abba, Father" (v. 6). Finally, as regards the body of Christ, we can distinguish two moments, so to speak: that of its realization and, as it were, its structuration, and that of its sanctification and animation (see, on this, Theodore of Mopsuestia, *Ritus baptismi*). All through, it is the work of the Holy Spirit to effect and bring to pass *within us*, in succeeding ages, what Christ did and established *for us* on a single occasion, at the time of his Incarnation. (In this connection, we may compare what theologians sometimes call the objective and the subjective Redemption, which is the application to men, the "effectuation in men", of the Redemption acquired by and in Christ.)

3. *Some practical applications*

Here I will touch on one or two problems often discussed which I believe can be clarified by what has just been said.

(a) *The duality of the sacraments of Baptism and Confirmation*

It is not easy to see the reason and nature of this duality, or what belongs strictly to Confirmation in contrast to Baptism, since the latter itself confers grace, and brings about the friendship of God and his presence within us. I personally am inclined to think that both the intimate connection and the duality of the two sacraments have to be seen together in the light of the duality of the Persons and missions, along with the unity of work, of Christ and the Holy Spirit. The Spirit comes to complete Christ's own work and the two moments of a single work are signified and effected, in the liturgy, in its own special manner, by two different sacramental actions, of which the second is related to the first.

(b) *The problem of Scripture and Tradition*

Tradition corresponds to the putting into effect of Christ's words and acts, and that is the work of the Holy Spirit living in the Church. According to the Gospel, he is to proclaim Christ beforehand in history and guide the apostles into all truth (John xiv. 26; xvi. 12–15). There is a *post pentecostal* understanding of Christ's acts and words and of the whole of Scripture. It is, of course, not a new creation, for the Spirit speaks only what he has heard, but he hears and keeps it better than men and, by continually recalling it to their minds, makes them advance ever further in the knowledge of Christ's truth. We see that in the very lifetime of the apostles and St. John himself testifies to it (cf. ii. 22; xii. 16); it is the continuous actualization, in the Church of the word uttered once and for all by God.

This applies to the Church's Tradition as such and also to our spiritual life as individuals. It happens that, in prayer, God himself speaks within us a passage of Scripture, of the psalms or the Gospel, or of some spiritual work. In the celebration of the liturgy especially, it happens at times that some passage is not just a mere sentence or an objective statement of a truth rightly understood, but it is something uttered by God to me in the depths of the soul, and so becomes in me fervour, life, power, fulness and certitude, far beyond any purely intellectual grasp. We have only to think, say, of Pascal's experience, of which his Memorial is the abiding witness; or, especially, of the saints. In this connection, see *The Ascent of Mount Carmel* of St. John of the Cross, book II, ch. 31. All this is to be ascribed to the working of the Holy Spirit.

(c) *The "spiritual" sects*

There are certain spiritual movements—some of us may have had some contact with them—which set forth practices to obtain guidance from the Holy Spirit. There is nothing wrong there, but where they do go astray is in not relating this guidance to Christ's work, to the *given and definite* thing, done once and for all, which is the positive and historical work of Christ—the Gospel, the apostolic doctrine, the Church. Now, if the Holy Spirit is really at work and if it is wrong to make for the Church as an institution claims so exclusive, so purely legalistic, as to leave no room for the action of the Spirit, it would be an error at least as great and certainly more dangerous (the worst excesses have tried so to justify themselves) to appeal to the Holy Spirit and to expect everything directly from him, while ignoring the positive datum, derived from Christ's institution, which it is precisely the mission of the Spirit to make real and actual in us.

In so saying, I am thinking of all the "illuminisms" which lack any external rule, the various "spiritual" sects following one after the other throughout the Church's history. To some extent, also, this applies to a thing good in itself and, in some ways, productive of good, but yet which gives rise to certain doubts, namely, the Moral Rearmament Movement of Dr. Buchman.

The danger to which I allude has always been present in substance practically from the beginning of Christianity. The happenings of Pentecost and the charismata of the infant Church left such a strong impression on the first Christian generations as to lead to the idea of a Christianity and a Church *of the Holy Spirit* involving a purely spiritual conception of Christ and the life of the Church. We can see this from the first epistle of St. Paul to the Corinthians, chapters 12 to 14, and also from the attitude taken up by St. John and St. Ignatius of Antioch. These both insist on the fact that the Christ-Spirit was the same being as the Christ incarnate, and that the Lord of the Church, who works in it by his Spirit, is the same who was born, suffered, died and rose. In short, Pentecost is the continuation of Easter and Christmas, and is closely bound up with these decisive events. What the Holy Spirit does is simply to interpret the mystery of Christ, of history, and to bring home its fulness to men. This idea so dominates the mind of St. John that it furnishes a key to the understanding of his Gospel. In the Apocalypse, the Spirit of prophecy is identical with the testimony of Jesus (xix. 10; cf. John xv. 26; xvi. 13–15; 1 John iv. 3 especially). Consequently, there neither is, nor can be, a "Church of the Spirit", a Christianity derived from interior inspiration, other than the Church of the Incarnate Word, a Christianity of the one historically given positive Revelation, of Christ come in the flesh, of the apostles and the institutional Church begun with them.

3. *For the Glory of the Father*

From whatever aspect it be considered, the ultimate reason for the order of the "Economy", of God's plan of salvation, is to be sought in the nature of God's own life in his Trinity of Persons. The reason of all we have just seen as regards the relation of the work of the Holy Spirit to that of Christ is that the Holy Spirit is the Spirit of Christ. Consider the terms used of him in the New Testament—*Spirit of Christ* (1 Peter i. 11; Romans viii. 9), *Spirit of the Lord* (Acts v. 9; viii. 39; 2 Cor. iii. 17–18), *Spirit of Jesus* (Christ) (Acts xvi. 17 Phil. i. 19; Romans viii. 9–11), *Spirit of his Son* (Gal. iv. 6).

We find, also, that the Spirit is sent us at the prayer of Christ (John xiv. 16), in his name (xiv. 26), by him (xv. 26; cf. xix. 30; xx. 22; Apoc. xxi. 6). We must go still further and say that the Holy Spirit "proceeds" from the Son. St. John says that he proceeds from the Father (xv. 26), but also that he "receives" of the Son (xvi. 15), and shows us the river of living water, his usual image of the Holy Spirit, "proceeding" from the throne of God and from the Lamb, that is, from the Father and the Son (Apoc. xxii. 1). This point of doctrine reached its final precision and expression in the words *a Patre Filioque* in the Latin text of the Creed. The Greeks did not accept this formula; their Fathers preferred to say that the Holy Spirit "proceeds from the Father through the Son", and the Council held at Ferrara and Florence in 1438 and 1439 officially recognized that this formula, correctly interpreted, is really equivalent to the formula "proceeds from the Father and the Son". On the strength, then, of this assurance, let us join together gladly in the faith of the Fathers, Eastern as well as Western. It is in communion with Athanasius, Hilary, Chrysostom, Augustine, Cyril of Alexandria, as with the apostles themselves, that we will sing our Credo at Chartres, and that we shall exert ourselves once more today to gain an understanding, as far as possible, of the mystery of the Spirit of Pentecost.

This Spirit relates himself wholly to Christ, and comes from him. In fact, Pentecost is the final mystery of the Christological cycle; there is no cycle proper to the Holy Spirit. It is the completion of Easter, that is of the work of the Incarnate Word, but brought about by a new Person sent by the Father and the Son.

Since he is sent by the Father and the Son, and proceeds from them, the Holy Spirit, with all that he works in us, is wholly relative to the Son and the Father. We end our Introits and our psalms with the doxology: Glory be to the Father, and to the Son, and to the Holy Ghost. The Church of antiquity preferred to say: Glory be to the Father, through the Son, in the Holy Ghost, so making the manner of praise and glorification correspond to the order of the "procession" (the living flow of being) and of the mission of the Persons of the Son and the Spirit. God's plan is for all things to go back to the Father according to the order in which they come from him and this includes the whole of creation and, more especially, the human creation made to the image of God.

We have seen above that the glory of the Son is to refer everything to the Father in loving and strictly filial obedience to his Will. The Son, too, is himself "glorified" by fulfilling in men God's will for their salvation through his Pasch, that is, his death, resurrection and sending of his Spirit to his followers. Likewise, the Holy Spirit, the Spirit of the Son, finds his glory in fulfilling in us the work of Christ and so, through Christ, of the Father. The glory of God is the Church, mankind united to Christ by faith and love, become his body by Baptism and the Eucharist, a single body bound together in filial obedience and self-giving, living in holiness by his Spirit. Thus it sings glory to the Father *in unitate Spiritus Sancti,* as we say at the end of the prayers in the Missal, and also in the final doxology of the Canon of the Mass, with which we end this first meditation of our pilgrimage: "Through him [Christ], O Lord, thou dost ever create all these good things, sanctify, vivify and bless them and give them to us. Through him, and with him, and in him, be to thee, God the Father Almighty, in the unity of the Holy Ghost, all honour and glory for ever and ever. Amen".

AT PENTECOST THE CHURCH WAS GIVEN ITS LAW AND ITS SOUL

The divine dynamism, which is the work of the Holy Spirit, flowed through Christ in his Pasch; and, after him, it flows through the Church. The Abbé Nautin has pointed out that the original formula of the profession of faith at Baptism was, "I believe in the Holy Spirit in the holy Church."

The world came into existence, its form was moulded, life sprang up at the beginning, through the creative dynamism. The book of Genesis shows us the spirit of God brooding, in some way, over what was about to be (Gen. I. 2), and then it says of Adam: "God formed man of the slime of the earth, and breathed into his face the breath of life, and man became a living soul" (ii. 7). With Christ there begins a new and definite phase of the spiritual history of mankind, for Christ is the new Adam, animated not by being breathed upon for the life of earth, but by a "spiritual" breathing for the life of heaven (cf. I Cor. xv. 45). Further, just as Adam was given, in Eve, a help like unto himself, drawn moreover from him (Gen. ii. 21 sq.), so Christ, the second and spiritual Adam, received for his spouse the Church, which the Fathers see coming out of his side while he was in the sleep of death, symbolized by the water and blood, and to which the Lord communicates his Spirit to enable it to live by the same spiritual and heavenly life as he does (cf. John xix. 33–34; xx. 21–23; Acts ii). The Lord had settled the elements which were to make up the Church in the course of his public life. He instituted the apostolic office and made choice of the Twelve, giving the primacy to Peter. He made known the mystery of God as proclaimed in the Gospel; he instituted the sacraments. Thus, gradually, the structure of the Church was built up. Then, at the end of the Paschal fifty days, he gave it its living principle, the Holy Spirit. This it is which is our present subject of meditation, and there are two aspects to be considered; for, at Pentecost, the Church received, with the Holy Spirit, both its law and its soul.

The Church received its law

The Jewish Pentecost, corresponding in date with the Christian, was a feast of the first fruits of the harvest (cf. Leviticus xxiii; Exodus xxiii. 16; xxxiv. 12). But the feasts of the Jewish liturgy, as Father Daniélou makes clear, did not refer exclusively to the seasons and the order of nature; they were, besides, and even mainly, a commemoration of the great acts of the economy of salvation wrought by God for his people. The Pasch, for instance, besides being a feast of springtime, was a commemoration of

B

God's great act of delivering Israel from its captivity in Egypt. Likewise, Pentecost was something other than the feast of first fruits. As the Law had been given to the people of God the third month after leaving Egypt (Exodus xix. 1)—we could even say, on the ground of certain indications in the Bible, the 50th day after the first Pasch—Pentecost came to be considered a memorial of the giving of the Law on Sinai. This idea, already held by the Jews at the time of the apostles, was expressly received into the liturgy of the Synagogue shortly before the catastrophe of the year 70. Nowadays, our Jewish brethren, who keep the Pasch on a different day from us, celebrate Pentecost, fifty days after the Pasch, as the feast both of first fruits and of the giving of the Law. They call it, in fact, "the feast of the gift of the Law", and on it they read the account of the promulgation of the Decalogue.

The Fathers of the Church were fond of alluding to this correspondence, which even St. Luke in the Acts does not notice (1). It is, in fact, highly significant, as we are now to see.

What is the law? It is the order authoritatively decreed by the head of a community, and giving it its form of life, its rule of collective living; and so it harmonises and adjusts the conduct of individuals to make of them a social unity. It is at once clear that when, as is the case with the Church, we are dealing with a community whose aim is salvation, whose life is of the spirit, the law is much more than something imposed by external force. As regards Christians, this law is chiefly the Holy Spirit in their hearts. That is St. Paul's meaning when he says, speaking of the community (Church) of Corinth: "You are an open letter from Christ, promulgated through us; a message written not in ink, but in the spirit of the living God, with human hearts, instead of stone, to carry it" (2 Cor. iii. 3). St. Thomas Aquinas, who spoke with precision and was not in the habit of giving a pious or "edifying" twist to his words, says the same, that the new law, of the Messianic era which is the present, is principally the grace of the Holy Spirit (*Summa Theol.* Ia–IIae, q. 106, art. I). Let us examine what this really means.

God's plan, which aims at building up the Body of Christ, is realized through the Holy Spirit. You know how a body is gradually formed by the operation of an interior law of organization which, starting from a first germ, small enough but rich in its consequences, fashions the various organs and assigns each its place so that, at the end of nine months, the infant is born with all that makes up the human organism. The same principle of organization subsequently ensures the concurrence of all the functions, organs and limbs in the unity of a single life. Now, what the life of a man or his soul does for his body, the Holy Spirit does for the body of Christ, of which he is the inmost law of its being, and he follows the two stages we have just described. His action starts out from Christ, and he distributes all the different gifts which come from Our Lord; and, in addition, he makes the gifts he places in each person work together in unity.

The Holy Spirit forms and distributes the organs of the Body of Christ

First of all, he distributes to individuals and imparts to them interiorly the numerous gifts flowing from the riches of Christ, our Head. St. Paul, describing the work of the Holy Spirit in forming the mystical Body, enumerates the different and complementary gifts he distributes (1 Cor. xii. 4–11, an important passage which should be read here, and the following). In one highly charged verse, the last of the second epistle to the Corinthians (xii. 13), St. Paul expresses the proper function of the Holy Spirit by a Greek word, Κοινωνία, which may be rendered either "communion" or "communication". Both translations are correct, for, in the New Testament, Κοινωνία signifies communication and communion by participation in a single source of good, which, in this context, is Christ in his Pasch. The special function of the Holy Spirit is to communicate to all and each something of the fulness of Christ; hence, the saying of St. Irenaeus, "In it [the Church] has been set up the communication of Christ, that is to say the Holy Spirit" (*Adv. Haereses*, iii. 24, 1). Here we come back to, and could extend, what we said in the last chapter about the relation of the work of the Holy Spirit to that of Christ. Christ has established for all men a salvation which is objective and collective, an objective treasure of grace and truth; and the Holy Spirit communicates to us and makes our own, imparts to us interiorly and personally, something of this treasure.

This he is able to do precisely because he is the Holy Spirit. Once again, his *role* in regard to us is explained by *his own nature*, the "economy" by the "theology". The Holy Spirit as he is, in God, the final term of the communication of life from the Father —which communication constitutes the Trinity—is also God's innermost communication to man. St. Paul repeatedly expresses his function by the fact that he is given "into our hearts", that is to say into the inmost depths of the personality (Gal. iv. 6; Rom. v. 5; viii. 27; 2 Cor. iii. 2 sq.; cf. Eph. i. 18; iii. 17). It is not without reason that he is spoken of by Scripture as the gift proper to the Messianic era (cf. Acts ii. 17 sq.), for he is the source of the inner renewal characteristic of the New Covenant (cf. Jer. xxxiii. 31 sq.; Ez. xxxvi. 25 sq.; cf. Isaias xxxii. 15 sq.; xliv. 3–5). We speak of the Holy Spirit in particular as dwelling in us, of man as the temple of the Holy Spirit (cf. 1 Cor. iii. 16; vi. 1;); in fact, he is so deeply present in the depths of the soul as the indwelling God that, in a manner, he works within us our most personal and inward acts, he prays in us (Rom. viii. 26). The really fervent soul desires that God himself should make himself its prayer, joy, peace and love to such a degree that it should no longer be the soul that acts, but God. This presence of God and his all-embracing action is promised to us at the very end, in the Kingdom of God which will be wholly interior and where God will be "all in all" (1 Cor. xv. 28); that will be the work of the Holy Spirit finally perfected. But, as St. Paul says, we already have the first fruits of the Spirit (cf. Eph. i 14; 2 Cor. i. 22; v. 5). For that reason, the Christian life, which is "life in the Spirit", implies even now a degree of inwardness, making the Holy Spirit, dwelling in us, the actual source of our spiritual life, so that it is not easy to distinguish what comes from him and what is ours. St. Paul says that, by the Spirit of adoption, we cry, Abba, Father; and also that the Spirit sent into our hearts himself utters this cry (cf. Rom. viii. 15, Gal. iv. 6; and see Rom. viii. 16).

The Holy Spirit, the source of communion in unity

God's plan is to go from unity to unity by way of what is manifold. It is the Holy Spirit who brings this plan to fulfilment; and so, having seen how he communicates to many a variety of different gifts taken from the one treasure which is Christ's, we will go on to see him bringing this multitude to the unity of a single body, that of Christ developed, "fulfilled", in us (Eph. i. 23). These gifts so imparted are destined, St. Paul tells us, for the benefit of all (1 Cor. xii. 17), for the building up of the body of Christ (Eph. iv). The Holy Spirit then, who is the indwelling law of the distribution of life to the different members, is, besides, the law of their communion in unity.

A unity which comes from within

It is a question of unity between persons (cf. Pascal: "a body formed of thinking members", frag. 473). In that body which is the Church, and which we call "mystical", not as meaning nebulous or unreal but as indicating its difference from the physical bodies of this world, the unity of its members cannot be one of fusion; it must be unity of communion. It is constituted by an order within living beings of identical nature, an inward order that gathers up the entire spiritual person, and at the deepest level, into total allegiance to faith and love and that moulds each and all according as the one divine life is actualized in them. That is what the Holy Spirit brings about in us, according to Christ the sole exemplar and for the sake of the one Father of us all. Glory be to the Father, through the Son, in the Holy Spirit, said the early Fathers; and many said, in equivalent terms, Glory be to the Father and to the Son with the Holy Spirit (e.g. St. Hippolytus). That is what the Church is for, and its profound unity.

As regards faith, the foundation of all that is Christian, the Holy Spirit it is who moves us inwardly so as to "use all the same language, with no divisions among you, but restored to unity of mind and purpose" (1 Cor. i. 10); and this not only "within", by a vague sentimental aspiration without any exact obligation, but also outwardly, in the Church, in conformity with the apostolic and ecclesiastical form of faith held and professed by all.

This comes about, however, not in any entirely external way, as though by a sort of regimentary compulsion, but from within, through a universal and intimate union of souls.

The Church is no more a military establishment than a soviet or a parliament. In this connection, I could easily quote the Fathers, but, instead, here is an excellent example from the present, all the more telling in that the person in question was put to death for what he said. The Communist police said to a Chinese woman they were questioning: "You are all the same, you Catholics; either you keep silence or you say the same thing. That means you must have some secret organization. What is it?"

Shou Yi answered: "If you really want to know, our secret organization is the Holy Spirit. In Manchuria, Africa, America and here, Catholics all believe and say the same thing, because it is the same Spirit that dwells in our hearts and speaks by our lips" (Monsterlet, *Les martyrs de Chine parlent,* Paris, 1953, p. 141).

What about unity of action? Look at a hive, or else read what Maeterlinck says. The bees are governed by an instinct, acting from necessity and unconsciously, which strictly controls, without leaving any scope for chance or whim, all their acts. It is the same with the other animals; lacking a personal destiny dependent on what they do, they have no freedom. We, however, made to the image of God and so personally immortal and free, are to bring about, consciously and through love, something analogous to what the bees do—namely, to form a single body, the body of Christ. The unity of mankind—still more, the spiritual unity of men in Christ—has to be established, not by physical fusion and loss of personality, but by that love in which, by uniting himself to others, each becomes most truly himself. The Body of Christ is not a hive, but a city of free men, willingly harmonising themselves to one another in love. There is, indeed, an external law whose function is to assist us in this; the Church has one, just as the State has. St. Thomas defines it as what authority lays down in view for the common good. So the Church has its rules and its law of living in unison. But its deepest law, its inmost spring of action, is the Holy Spirit, who causes us to keep unity of spirit in the bond of peace (Eph. iv. 3).

The Holy Spirit, through the love he instils, breaks our bondage to egoism, to our private inclinations, to the spirit of contradiction and distrust (Eph. ii. 2), to the spirit of the world of which St. Paul speaks (1 Cor. ii. 12), which is a spirit of self-centredness, exclusiveness, withdrawal from others. The spirit of Christ, on the other hand, is one of communion—see the magnificent programme of its practice in Rom. xii. 3–16—"no want of unity in the body, all the different parts of it to make each other's welfare their common care" (1 Cor. xii. 25). The Spirit of love impels us from within to the service of others and harmony with them, in short, to communion. Cajetan, in his commentary on St. Thomas, says that the sin of schism is the exact contrary of the charity given to us by the Holy Spirit, which moves us to act, not as single wholes isolated from each other, self-sufficient monads, but as parts of members of a larger whole. That is the fullest and most exact meaning of the word "Catholic", which comes from the Greek Καθ' ὅλον, meaning "according to the whole". To be Catholic is to act fraternally, to act in the spirit of the Church; it is, in Moehler's words, "to think and will in unison with all". All this goes to show how the Holy Spirit is truly the law of Christianity, and how the Church, in receiving him at Pentecost, received its law.

The Holy Spirit acting in the world

The Holy Spirit, being a living Person, dwells and acts in the innermost being of all who are really Christians; and so the effect proper to him is to bring together to unity and to the realization of God's plan men and things widely apart and unconnected. This is abundantly illustrated both in past history and in present experience. For my part, I have had undoubted evidence of it, and it fills me with wonder and joy. Whenever we look into the life of a saint, or indeed the spiritual history of anyone, it is amazing to see how seemingly chance occurrences turn out in the end to have been, as it were, prepared long before for some purpose, and that by a variety of circumstances often at first bewildering. I have seen it often in my own life. On numerous occasions it has happened that I have worked alone and silently on precisely those subjects on which it turned out that persons unknown to me needed enlightenment, or whose outcome corresponded exactly, even in verbal expression, to the ideas that others, whom I did not know or who were at the time out of contact with me, were themselves developing. But, surely, everyone who loves God can testify to happenings in his life, to help received just when needed, in conditions quite unforeseeable. And if we take as an example the modern oecumenical movement, it is extraordinary how the desire for Christian unity, and action for its furtherance, have come into being at the same time practically everywhere, among people unknown to one another or divergent in many ways, rather as all nature in the Spring begins to germinate, to flower and to sing as if at the secret signal of some orchestral conductor, himself unseen.

This special work of the Holy Spirit, who is the interior law of the apostolate, is clearly manifest in the wonderful coincidences we notice occurring. Seemingly fortuitous, they are in reality brought about secretly by him who fills the whole world and makes it all sing one song to God (cf. Introit for Pentecost). I know a number of these, both in history and in my own experience. One of them is recorded in Acts viii. 26–39, which is used in place of an Epistle for the Mass of the Thursday after Pentecost. It happened on the road to Gaza, where Philip the deacon was travelling in obedience to an interior inspiration, not knowing of the "coincidence" in store for him, and that he would meet, as we meet someone unexpectedly in a tube station or on coming from a lecture, someone he would bring to belief in Christ. Any priest or missioner will affirm that the work of the apostolate is largely dependent on chance circumstances and coincidence; but the director of all these is the Holy Spirit.

Interior communion . . . and hierarchical functions

All that has been said above about the Holy Spirit as the force impelling to communion and the internal law governing it is to be seen in the Church born at Pentecost as described in the Acts of the Apostles. There, the early Church appears to be literally fashioned by special interventions of the Holy Spirit. This can be easily seen by reading carefully the text of the Acts, and noting every passage where the Spirit is said to act. And the following verses, which contain the fullest description of the life of the primitive Church, illustrate in striking fashion our present subject: "These [the first Christians] occupied themselves continuously with the apostles' teaching, their fellowship in the breaking of bread, and the fixed times of prayer" (ii. 42); "there was one heart and soul in all the company of believers . . . everything was shared in common" (iv. 32); "the Church became firmly established, guided by the fear of God, and filled with encouragement by the Holy Spirit" (ix. 31).

Consider a moment the first of these verses. It proclaims briefly what goes to make up the Church in itself and is present wherever the Church is, whether it be the universal Church, a diocese, a parish, or a smaller community such as a study circle. Always, we find these three elements which make up the ecclesiastical communion: a community in faith, governed by the apostolic teaching; a community of service, of corporate assemblies, of mutual fraternal assistance; and, finally, a community of prayer formed principally by collective participation in the one eucharistic bread. To these three elements there correspond the three functions characterizing, formerly, the people of God in the Old

Testament, and continuing in the Church, from the time of Christ and the apostles, under the impulse of the Holy Spirit. These are the *Magisterium*, the spiritual government of the various communities, and the priestly function.

These are the three essential hierarchical functions, without which the Church would not be fully present. But the action of the Holy Spirit along these lines produces an effect so profound that it can be expressed only by the words used in the Creed, *communio sanctorum*, which are to be taken, at one and the same time, in the two senses of communion in sacred things, the sacraments and the Eucharist (the *sancta*), and communion of saints, of Christians in a state of friendship with God (the *sancti* and *sanctae*). Once again, it is the Holy Spirit, the inward law of the Church and the Christian life, who establishes between all the faithful this profound communion, so much greater than that part of it we may perceive or experience in the visible life of the Church. We all of us hold the same doctrines, but the Holy Spirit establishes, in our hearts, so profound a communion of faith that, for example, the faith of parents or godparents is what counts, and is effective, in infant Baptism; the Holy Spirit is the real link between them and the child as yet without thought and speech.

In Christ, and through the Spirit, there is set up a communication between person and person. We celebrate the same Eucharist, but it is the Spirit who, by means of the body and blood of Christ, vivifies and sanctifies us, and makes us one body with Christ (so John vi. 64, as understood by many of the Fathers). We pray one for the other, we share their burdens, but the Holy Spirit is, in reality, the mysterious bond of this Communion of Saints, and makes the prayers and works of each redound to the benefit of all. If the Body is one by reason of its soul, the Holy Spirit, there can take place through that same Spirit a kind of exchange or supplying of deficiencies. So it was that St Teresa of the Child Jesus could, by prayer and penance performed in her convent at Lisieux, assist the work of missionaries far away in China or Indochina. The Church has a firm belief in the power of the prayer of contemplatives for those in the forefront of the battle.

Have we a real faith in the Communion of Saints, in the Holy Spirit? Are we convinced of the existence of that marvellous aspect of the mystery of the Church that far transcends what we directly perceive, and that it derives from the Holy Spirit its bond, interior law and soul? He is present in all the faithful, in unique and sovereign fashion; and, without infringing upon the autonomy and inner freedom of the person, he joins all together in a unity transcending time and place and everything else that divides men. What St. Paul says in the Epistle to the Romans, viii. 35–38, should be read in this light, in reference to the effects of the Spirit.

Permissible differences and essential unity

The problem is familiar enough; it is one which often troubles the Hierarchy (cf. Cardinal Feltin's Lenten pastorals for 1951 and 1952). We are, each of us, different, very much so; and that is, in some ways, an excellent thing. We have our own views, sometimes very divergent ones, in art, economics, politics, and even, to some extent, in theology. That is quite legitimate, and no one will dispute our right. But we have to be careful. These differences could degenerate into divisions, and lead to bitter and barren disputes, which would not only be a frightful hindrance to the Church's action, but might even strike at the heart of charity, its very law, and so cause real scandal.

This all goes to show that there are two things to which we must be particularly attentive. I shall deal with them very briefly here; they are a special subject of study, which needs to be fully treated. The first is to place, *effectively,* in the forefront, above all that divides us, the great things we have in common: faith, prayer, the Eucharist, Christ himself; and, in proportion to our avowed differences in temporal and human concerns, to cultivate more intensely unity in the great activities of the Church and the great realities of the Christian life we have just been considering. It is a matter of fostering the community of faith, of mutual help in charity, and of prayer and the sacraments, apart from which there is no Church at all. The second thing is to try and develop, in obedience to the Spirit of communion, the ability to adapt oneself to others, by becoming aware of, and mastering, our possessiveness, personal predilections, obstinacy and that attachment to our own opinions that makes impossible any understanding of others or communication with them. We have to becomes persons "in communion", and that by a deepening of our spiritual awareness, quite a different thing from mere pliability.

Otherwise, we should have no part in the Spirit of Pentecost. We should be, to our utter loss, excommunicating ourselves from the truth and from the celebration of this Whit-Sunday on the road to Chartres.

The Church received its soul

In the preceding pages, there often recurred the words "soul" or "animation", since the law received by the Church at Pentecost in the Holy Spirit is like the internal law of a living organism, and so very close to what we call the soul. In this second part of our meditation, we treat of the same thing, but in a different aspect. Whereas before we considered the actual life of the Church, its physiology, as it were, we now come to its inner constitution, the law of its being—its internal morphology, if you like. There seem to me to be three points we have to pay special attention to if we want to understand how Pentecost was decisive in the realization of the plan of God's grace which was to set up, in the world, a Body of sanctity and salvation, the Church of holiness.

God himself, the Holy Spirit, gives himself to the Church to be its soul

It is often most rewarding to follow out some particular subject from the book of Genesis right up to the Apocalypse making, as it were, a vertical cutting through the strata of the revealed word. If we use this method to study the gradual revelation and realization of God's dwelling among men (the Temple theme), or the progressive revelation of the Holy Spirit, we find this: under the Old Covenant, before the coming of Christ, God *intervened* actively in the life of his people; the Holy Spirit is seen, generally, as the power God makes use of in raising up and actuating the leaders of the people (Moses, Joshua, the Judges, David, *et al.*), in calling and inspiring the prophets—the Holy Spirit is truly he "qui locutus est per prophetas", as we sing in the Creed. It is certainly the case that the period of the Law saw numerous souls admirable in a religious and moral aspect, and in an advanced state of union with God. Yet, as St. Paul, says, the Law could not bring anyone to perfection (Heb. vii. 19); and it was a sign of this that Moses died in view of the Promised Land, without being able to enter it. The virtues and the justice of the people of the Old Testament were perfectly real; they were highly charged with faith and hope, but they were powerless to bring their possessors to God or the heaven he inhabits. They disposed men interiorly in conformity with the will of God, but did not *fully* unite them to God, since he had not yet given and committed himself *completely*. It is the teaching of Tradition, based on the New Testament (as, for instance, on 1 Peter iii. 19 and iv. 6), that the just of the Old Testament had to wait for the coming of Christ before they could go to Heaven—that is the meaning of the descent into hell of the Creed. They had, undoubtedly, received God's gifts, but God himself had not yet given himself with these gifts and, so long as he was not personally joined to his gifts, these, however holy, could not bring men to gain him, the Giver.

The new and decisive element brought in by Pentecost—itself the consequence and completion of the coming of the Word in human form—is that God now is personally and entirely given along with the gifts of grace and that, henceforth, these are invested with full efficacy, enabling us to reach heaven and complete communion with God himself. We have only to see the way in which the newness of the Christian, by contrast with the Jewish, dispensation is presented by St. Paul (2 Cor. iii; Heb. iii and viii. 10), by St. Peter in his discourse on the feast of Pentecost (Acts ii. 16 sq.), and by St. John (i. 17; vi. 31–33). All through St. John, the Acts and the Epistles of St. Paul, we find it asserted that we have passed from the preparation to the reality, received, at least in pledge, the supreme gift beyond which there can be none other ("new and eternal Testament"), since it is God himself come to us in the flesh and given in the Person of the Holy Spirit. Look again at Col. i. 12–14; indeed, almost any page of the New Testament bears abundant witness to this.

In short, at Pentecost, the fiftieth day and completion of the Pasch, the Person of the Holy Spirit was finally given to the Church and, in it, to its members, as the moving principle of their life, the root of the tree of grace bearing the fruits of Paradise (the Fathers see in the Holy Spirit the real tree of life).

This fact underlies the idea of the Fathers and the whole Christian tradition that the Holy Spirit is the soul of the Church. St. Augustine, in particular, is always recurring to it, especially in his Pentecost sermons (*Sermo* 267, 4, P.L., vol. 38, col. 1231; 268, 2, col. 1232). What the soul is for man's body, he says, the Holy Spirit is for the Body of Christ, which is the Church; and as the Holy Spirit overshadowed the Virgin Mary to form in her the temporal individual body of Christ, so he was given to the Church at Pentecost to make it into the spiritual, "communional" Body of the Lord.

The Holy Spirit, then, is the soul of the Church; and, indeed, in two aspects important and easy to distinguish. He is, first of all, the *animating soul,* the source of all the activities concerning or aiming at holiness and salvation, activities peculiar to the Church and to the individual Christian. He is the source of my prayer (Rom. viii. 26), my loving (Rom. v. 5), of all my virtues, such as they are (v. 16–25; Gal. v. 22 sq.); the source, too, of the acts by which the priesthood and the hierarchy sustain and guide the Body of Christ in the way of faith, grace and all that goes to make up the life of mutual charity we have already spoken of and will return to in a moment. Besides this, he is the *indwelling soul*; he not only acts in the Church, but dwells in it. The House of the Lord was not made just for him to gaze on its beauty, but to receive him as its guest. It is, in fact, precisely because he is its guest that it practises holiness and justice. We may recall, in this connection, the episode of Zachaeus (Luke xix. 1–10), which is used as the Gospel for the feast of the dedication of a Church because it expresses so well the mystery of God's indwelling; once he enters the soul, he stirs it up to works of justice and saves what had been lost. We find this mystery spoken of in John xiv. 15–17 23; 1 Cor. iii. 16; vi. 19; 1 John iii. 24; iv. 13–16, and elsewhere in the same Epistle.

As Christians, we have to look on the truths of Christianity and on the Church with the eye of faith. The Holy Spirit cannot be seen directly; that is why Christ likens him to the wind, whose effects can be perceived, but which is not seen with the eye (John iii. 8). He is Breath, he is Spirit. But, in faith, we are to venerate his real Presence within us, in our brethren and in the Church; and so we sing, in the Sequence of today's Mass, "Dulcis hospes animae".

St. Augustine's comparison is, however, not to be pressed too far. Every comparison, of course, has its limits, otherwise it would no longer be a comparison, but an expression of the thing in itself. Though the Holy Spirit is the soul animating and indwelling the Body of Christ, he does not make up, with this Body, a physical and substantial whole, as does our soul with our body. It is more a matter of a union between two realities, the Spirit and the Church, each having its own subsistence—a kind of marriage as if between two persons. In Scripture, the description of the Church as the Body of Christ is completed and, in a sense, corrected by its being also spoken of as the Bride of Christ. The two form one flesh, not by physical fusion—for then the Church would be strictly identical with Christ, impeccable even in its individual members and, like him, worthy of adoration—but by a spiritual union. The Church is the mystical Body of Christ. The Holy Spirit is its intimate guest, ever faithful, really given to it, close and enduring. He works in it without ceasing. It is not substantially united to him as Christ's humanity, taken from Mary, is united to the Word of God. The coming of the Holy Ghost at Pentecost was not, strictly speaking, an Incarnation. The Church has the Spirit, but it is not itself the Spirit. Yet the Pentecost gift is so entire, so perfect and complete, the Church is so dependent on the Spirit for all that it is, that the Fathers looked on the two passages of the Creed, [*credo*] *in Spiritum Sanctum* and *Sanctam Ecclesiam Catholicam*, as forming in reality one single article. They interpreted it as meaning "I believe in the Holy Ghost who unifies and sanctifies the Church, makes it Catholic and apostolic, making it thereby truly the Communion of saints and the Body of Christ, which, filling all things, is itself also 'fulfilled' in us and in the Church."

The Holy Spirit animates the individual person in relation to his special function within the body

The whole body is animated and indwelled by the Holy Spirit. But the Church is an organism, that is to say a body having different functions, where each part is animated in view of its own being and to perform its special work to the advantage of the whole. Consider the difference between a heap of branches that have been cut down and a living tree. The former is just wood weighing so much, of which one lot is as good as any other. The latter has an organic structure, composed of roots, trunk, main and subsidiary branches, leaves. Likewise, the Church is a body whose soul, the Holy Spirit, itself always one and the same, distributes his gifts to the different members according to their different functions, making some apostles, others pastors or doctors, and so on, so as to build up the Body of Christ to its full stature (cf. Eph. iv. 11; Romans xii. 4 sq.; 1 Cor. xii. 4–11; and Pius XII's encyclical *Mystici Corporis Christi* of 29 June 1942).

All this is of the greatest importance. The idea of the Church as an organism explains two things so necessary to grasp clearly and to bear in mind together whenever we speak of the Church, particularly when we try to estimate the respective roles of the ordinary faithful and of the Hierarchy. On the one hand, it is the whole Body which is indwelled, animated and in action. On the other, there exist, within the Body, hierarchical functions, which themselves are functions of service (Eph. iv. 16); and those who exercise them are animated and moved by the Spirit for this purpose. All the members are living and animated, but each according to what he is and to perform what he is called to do within the body. That is the law of the Church's being and which regulates its growth.

The ordinary faithful

They are all animated and made active by the Spirit. At Pentecost, it was not the apostles alone who received the Holy Ghost, but all the believers then existing and, as the Acts says (i. 15), assembled in the upper room to the number of about one hundred and twenty. All of them were animated and made active by the coming of the Spirit. You, too, are one of the cells of the Body. Do not say, or think, you have nothing to do in its regard, for you are to aid in its building. Your spiritual health, your vitality in Christ, are necessary to the Body's wholeness, to the realization of God's plan, and to the full health and vitality of all other Christians. No doubt, if a body receives some superficial wound, that is less serious than the loss of a hand or an eye; but still, it is not to be ignored. And what do you know of the place destined for you by Christ in the Body or in the history of salvation? Think, for instance, of Teresa of Lisieux or Charles de Foucauld, reckon the immensity of their spiritual influence, and you will realize that the Body of Christ is built up, that sacred history is accomplished by means of the most hidden gifts, distributed by the Spirit as he wills, in secret, given, indeed, as much to a solitary in the Sahara or a young nun in an unknown convent as to the Pontiffs who rule the Church. Once again, the reality which is the Church needs to be seen with the eye of faith. St. Paul (2 Cor. iii. 2–3) likens the Church to a letter from Christ, and it is by the gifts, often quite hidden, poured out by the Spirit of Pentecost, that this letter comes to be written.

At any rate, do not be discouraged by these outstanding examples if you are convinced that yours are not gifts or a vocation as sublime as these. Look at all the ways open to you by grace of serving others, and so of becoming a part of the great cathedral structure, if not as one of its columns or corner-stones, at least as one of its smaller stones. And just as you will soon see and admire at Chartres how the building has nothing superfluous, yet lacks nothing that is necessary, so among the "charisms", the spiritual gifts enumerated by St. Paul, there are some quite ordinary and modest ones (Romans xii. 4 sq.). As the Gospel tells us, a prayer, a glass of water given to another, are of value for the Kingdom of God. Such things as finding work for someone, distributing notices of meetings or periodicals, lending a book to an enquirer, encouraging one who falters—do not imagine these are of no account in God's eyes. The essential is not to have received an exceptionally high calling, but to correspond with the one you really have. The Holy Ghost is the moving force, and he knows the end in view.

The Hierarchy

The Church is, admittedly, made up of a number of very small stones, even grains of sand, but it must also have the larger elements to hold it together, corresponding to the foundations, framework, corner-stones in a material building. So it is that the Hierarchy, with its special calling and spiritual gifts, gives structural unity to the mystical Body of Christ. Consider how, in the Old Testament, the people of God was formed, animated and guided by the three essential functions of priest, king and prophet. We have noticed already the allusion to them in Acts ii. 42; and they are always present in every Christian community, from the universal Church as such right down to the smallest group, with the diocese and the parish in between.

Now, if we examine in the Acts of the Apostles what happened in the case of the primitive Church, which is the type or model for all times, we see, all through the book, the Church being built up through the co-operation of the Holy Ghost with these apostolic or hierarchical functions of preaching, of the administration of the sacraments, and of spiritual governance. This is developed at length in the final section of this work; but here we will give the most important references. They are Acts ix. 31; xx. 28 taken with xiv. 22; xiii. 1–4; v. 2 taken with v. 3; xv. 28. In all these, some activity of preaching or administration of the sacraments is ascribed jointly to the apostles and to the Holy Ghost. Likewise, in 2 Cor. iii. 2–3, the letter written by the apostle in his ministry is said, too, to be written by the Holy Ghost. John xv. 26–27 and Heb. ii. 3–4 refer to a combined witness of the apostles and the Holy Ghost (cf. Luke xxiv. 48–49 and Acts i. 8; 31–33; xvi. 14). Consider, too, the union of water and the Spirit in Baptism (John iii. 5); the remission of sins (John xx. 22–23), which shows that the Breath which wipes out sins passes through the channel of the apostles.

It is clear from all this that the Church is built up essentially by the co-operation of the Holy Spirit sent by Christ with the apostolic ministry he established—a kind of "con-celebration" of the visible ministry with the divine Person, as is so wonderfully expressed by the Eastern Liturgy.

This is the reason why all the more important acts of the ministry so instituted, that is of the hierarchical ministry, have the divine warrant in virtue of which, for example, when a priest absolves, it is truly God who absolves; when he consecrates the bread and wine, it is truly the power of Christ and the Last Supper that acts; when two Christians marry according to the laws of the Christian community, their "I will" is written in heaven and possesses a divine sacramental value. That is why the great doctrinal decisions (dogmatic definitions) or simply the unanimous affirmation of the episcopal body centred on Peter have the certainty and the value of God's own witness. It is not on account of the men who are ministers of the Church, but through the Holy Ghost who is the soul of the Church and of all that, in the Church, which belongs to its essence and concerns the actual building up of the people of God.

This explains the strong terms used by the earliest Fathers, martyrs too, like St. Irenaeus and St. Hippolytus (second and early third centuries), such as "Where the Church is, there is to be found the Holy Ghost and all grace" (Irenaeus, *Adv. Haereses*, P.G. vol. 7, col. 966).

Yet, for the reason already stated, the Church, or its Hierarchy, is not impeccable in the person of its human representatives; it is not even wholly guaranteed against error. For the Holy Ghost is not its soul in the sense of making with it one entity, united to it substantially as Christ's humanity is to the Word; the union is solely one of alliance. The Spirit and the Church are not absolutely one Person, but, so to speak, two persons, The alliance itself is assured, the gift is a real one—"I am with you [by my Spirit] unto the consummation of the world" (Mt. xxviii. 20)—and so, in what is essential, what constitutes the people of God, the Church cannot fail. The bride and the bridegroom are faithful to one another; but, though the latter is divine, the former is yet human. Along with her essential fidelity, divinely guaranteed by that of God himself, she still has the possibility, in each and all of the smaller details of her life, of falling short of the absolute of holiness and truth which is God. Her very fidelity is, indeed, under the impulse of the Spirit who is ever at hand to help her, one of a constant effort, accompanied with prayer, to co-operate to the utmost with the divine dynamism whose will it is, by means of the Church, to raise up the world.

Through the Holy Ghost, the Church is wholly bound up with heaven

The various shortcomings of the Church in history are familiar enough. We may even, at times, be inclined to exaggerate them. Today, however, we are to try to view with the eye of faith the

Church sprung from that first Pentecost, to perceive the truly divine sublimity of the Church which then received for its soul, its source of life and activity, no other and no less than the Spirit of God himself. Journet, in the second volume of his *Church of the Incarnate Word,* that monumental, highly technical, treatise, shows, in masterly fashion, how the Church is, in the world, that spiritual and holy society in which all achievement of value is bound up with God himself, as its ultimate source, and particularly with the Third Person, the Holy Ghost. If, as St. Paul says, no one can say from the heart "Jesus is the Lord", otherwise than in the Holy Spirit (1 Cor. xii. 3; cf. 1 John iv. 2–3), that is to say without a communication of grace freely and specifically made by the Holy Ghost, the same is true of every act of faith, of every true witness to God, of every act of love, of every true prayer, of all growth in holiness, of every act of virtue, of every act which the Church performs in communicating the grace of God. So it is that the eye of faith sees a divine history everywhere in process of becoming, within and concurrently with the world's earthly course, the history, indeed, of the people of God. We realize, too, that not a letter of it is spelt out, not a word formed, that the Holy Spirit, from the bosom of the Trinity, has not, secretly but sovereignly, written or uttered. "A power has gone out from me", said Christ at the moment when, in the crowd that pressed about him, a poor woman in the fulness of her faith was healed by touching his garment. Nothing that is holy ever takes place in the world except by participation in a power from the Holy Ghost, who gives it freely, in love.

So it is that the Church is wholly bound up with heaven, with the Trinity, its foundation and origin. "A unity proceeding from the divine immutability, and of the same nature as the heavenly mysteries" is what St. Cyprian, the martyr of Carthage, said of this Church in the middle of the third century. (*De Unitate,* ch. 6).

AT PENTECOST THE CHURCH SET OUT ON ITS MISSIONARY WORK

No sooner was its dynamism given to the living organism of the Church than it became a missionary body.

A mission is a particular task accepted with powers and grace to correspond. Christ had formulated the task in the words, "Go and make disciples of all nations" (Mt. xxviii. 19); "Go into the whole world and preach the Gospel to every creature" (Mark xvi. 15). Once again, the Holy Ghost completes his work, interiorises it within men and gives it living impulse; he brings to the mission received dynamism and grace. On every occasion when we see him at work, he brings a grace (charism) and a movement. As regards grace, see Luke i. 28 and 35; Acts iv. 31 and 33; vi. 3, 5 and 8. As regards movement, Acts ii. 4: "They were all filled with the Holy Ghost and they began to speak . . ."; iv. 31: "All then were filled with the Holy Ghost and began to speak the word of God boldly". As soon as the Spirit comes upon men, he moves them to bear witness to Christ.

Pentecost was not the beginning (birth) of the Church, if by that we mean its constitution or its setting up. That was done in the course of Christ's own life, inasmuch as he proclaimed the Gospel, revealed the Father, chose the twelve apostles, founded the primacy of Peter, inaugurated the sacraments (especially Baptism and the Eucharist), and so on. Pentecost was, precisely, the placing of the Church in the world.

It was placed in the world, both in the sense in which we speak of a child being brought into the world, when, after being formed in his mother's womb, he comes into the light of day and begins his own life; and somewhat in the sense, too, in which existentialism uses the expression "être à", as when M. Merleau Ponty defines the human situation as "être au monde à travers un corps". Certain it is that, with the coming of the Spirit at Pentecost, the Church was brought into the world. It appeared in full view before a great assembly of people from all the different countries enumerated in the Acts. It appeared with the highest possible degree of publicity, a publicity brought about by the Holy Ghost, the noise, the speaking with tongues, the enthusiasm. At the same time, the Church was sent to the world. The Pentecost force behind it was not for its own glory, but to mark the beginning of a mission universal in space and time, continuing till the return of the Son of Man. At Pentecost, the Church set out on its missionary work. Remember the Pentecost depicted on the tympanum at Vézelay. That is the image we should carry in our minds, the wind of Pentecost blowing in the garments of the apostles, so that we feel it driving them to all the various, at times strange, peoples there depicted.

Moreover, that is just what Our Lord proclaimed on his last appearance to his disciples: "That repentance and remission of sins should be preached in his name to all nations, beginning at Jerusalem. Of this you are witnesses. And behold I am sending down upon you the gift which was promised by my Father; you must wait in the city until you are clothed with power from on high" (Luke xxiv. 47–49); "He gave them orders, as he shared a meal with them, not to leave Jerusalem, but to wait there for the fulfilment of the Father's promise. You have heard it, he said, from my own lips; John's baptism, I told you, was with water, but there is a baptism with the Holy Spirit which you are to receive, not many days from this. . . . The Holy Spirit will come upon you, and you will receive strength from him; you are to be my witnesses in Jerusalem and throughout Judaea, in Samaria, yes, and to the end of the earth" (Acts i. 4–5, 8).

It has often been observed how St. Luke, in his Gospel, sets out the stages of Our Lord's life according to a geographical scheme, centred on Jerusalem and his gradual approach to the city, while in the Acts, writing at the same time under inspiration and with historical precision, he shows the history of the apostolic mission unfolding itself outwards from Jerusalem its centre, where took place Christ's Pasch, on through Judaea and Samaria, right across the world. We shall shortly draw out the significance of this for the New Testament idea of universalism. For the time being, we simply note that the Church born at Pentecost, the type of the Church of all times, is seen as essentially missionary.

At Pentecost, the Twelve were consecrated Apostles

Up to then, they had been disciples, they were just "the twelve". They had been singled out and instructed by Our Lord. But they were made "apostles" by the coming of the Holy Ghost, *apostoli per Spiritum,* if we may so punctuate Acts i. 2. This brings into their life two new elements—they are sanctified, and they are clothed with power.

They are sanctified

Jesus spoke of himself as "he whom the Father sanctified and sent into the world" (John x. 36). In what is sometimes called his sacerdotal prayer, and which I prefer to call his apostolic prayer (John xvi. 17), he prayed for his followers in these words to the Father: "I have given them thy message, and the world has nothing but hatred for them, because they do not belong to the world, as I too do not belong to the world . . . Keep them holy, then, through the truth; it is thy word that is truth. Thou hast sent me into the world on thy errand, and I have sent them into the world on my errand; and I dedicate myself for their sakes, that they too may be dedicated through the truth."

There are two points to be noted here:

(a) *Mission involves, from the outset, a sanctification*

We must realize fully what is implied in the Christian apostolate. An apostle is not the same as a "militant", or as a man of influence who gathers adherents round him. It is a lamentable abuse of language to speak, in the current fashion, of apostles of the press, of sport, of television and so on. It is essential to the apostle to be sanctified in the first place, before being sent out on a mission. This is not to say that he does not sanctify himself in and through the exercise of his mission. An apostle is a man of God, not merely a propagandist. He is a living element in God's plan of salvation, an emanation, as it were, of Christ himself, who said: "As the Father has sent me, so also I send you" (John xx. 21), and "As the Father has loved me, I also love you" (xv. 9). An apostle is one who hands on the saving love which, issuing from the Father's heart, passes through the incarnate Word, and is communicated to us by the Holy Spirit (Rom. v. 5). The mystery of the apostolate belongs to the order of holiness; and so St. Thomas Aquinas speaks of the personality of the apostles as being entirely penetrated and fashioned by the Holy Spirit, the Spirit of holiness.

It is, indeed, noteworthy that the two gifts which are to characterize the apostle, holiness and power, are precisely those which the Bible attributes as acts proper to the Holy Ghost—in the Old Testament, it is principally power; in the New, holiness as well as power.

(b) *This sanctification of the apostles is bound up with their having received the Word in obedience to the Father*

This it is which sanctifies the apostle (John xii. 48–50; xv. 3, 7; xvii. 3, 6–8, 14–19; cf. 1 John ii. 3 sq.). It is our loving obedience to the commandments of God which makes us consecrated temples in which he dwells (John xiv. 15–17, 21–24; xv. 3–4; 1 John iii. 24; cf. John xv. 9–10; xvii. 25–26; Exodus xix. 5–6). It is this fidelity in receiving and keeping the Word that makes apostles, makes them no longer servants but friends (John xv. 14–15). We have here an idea basically very much akin to that of "glory", which we spoke of in the first chapter. Our obedience to the Father consecrates us, sanctifies us, and constitutes our true glory at the same time as it procures his. It is, too, the apostolate, since this is the service which brings about the realization of the plan of God's grace.

They are clothed with power

This is one of the characteristics most often emphasised both in Scripture and Tradition (with Acts i. 8, see Luke xxiv. 49;

Acts iv. 33, x. 38; Rom. xv. 13, 19; I Cor. ii. 4–5; I Thess. i. 5). There is no true witness, no apostle, without a certain kind of vigour, assurance, spiritual power, which in Scripture is connected with the Spirit of God.

Indeed, if we consider what the apostles, Peter for example, were before and what they were after Pentecost, we are confronted with a total transformation, in view of the very simple narration given by the relevant passages. Before, they were braggarts, jealous of their privileges, inconstant, apprehensive of what men might say, timid, uncertain. Even after the resurrection, we come across them engaged once more in their former occupations (after all, they had to live) and disconcerted by Our Lord's appearances; or else, as on the very morning of the ascension, exuberantly optimistic after a month of such visitations, and expecting some great messianic exhibition of a purely external and worldly character. Then the Spirit comes. They speak with power and certainty; they are positive and resourceful, undeterred by the most imposing acts of authority or even by punishment inflicted; they confront unflinchingly a whole series of new situations.

Veni, Sancte Spiritus. How much we have need of him to become truly apostles.

Many of those in this pilgrimage of ours are to receive the sacrament of Confirmation. What is likely to happen, or will anything happen at all? We are not to expect any mighty disturbance, tongues of fire or the like, apart from the usual storm that occurs at Chartres at this time. But we do, most certainly, expect the Holy Spirit, his sanctification and his power.

Whoever tries seriously to enter into the liturgy and the theology of Confirmation will find himself enveloped in the apostolic and pentecostal atmosphere of which Scripture speaks. For my part, what strikes me particularly are the two following features which correspond perfectly to those we have just been studying—there is the aspect of consecration of God's temple (sanctification), and the aspect of communication of power for conflict and for bearing witness. The conflict in question is, of course, the messianic and apostolic one we are to conduct to be really witnesses of God, men who further, in however slight degree, the realization of his plan of grace in the world. It is of this that we will now speak, in connection with catholicity considered as one of the fruits of Pentecost.

The coming of the Holy Ghost laid the foundation of the Church's universality

Pentecost is the feast of this universality. Think, once again, of the tympanum of Vézelay, which expresses this so well; think, too, of the sign of tongues.

Hebert, in chapter 9 of his *Trône de David* (Paris, Aubier), shows that the Old Testament was not without a genuine universalist outlook, more pronounced indeed at the time of the exile and subsequently, but present and signified in the most ancient of its narratives, such as the story of Abraham. But, he goes on to say, this universalism was inseparable from the idea of Jerusalem as the centre to which all nations were to flow who had been gained over to the worship of the true God. That is perfectly true, provided that the coming of the Gentiles to Jerusalem be not interpreted in a too narrowly material and geographical sense. Still, the fact is, and it seems to have always been the ideal of the Jewish Christians, that the conversion of the Gentiles was envisaged as their conversion to Judaism, to the Jewish law and practices, and that it implied an admission of Israel as God's peculiar people, set apart for the worship of Jahve.

Christ, however, had said to the Samaritan woman: "Believe me, woman, the time is coming when you will not go to this mountain, nor yet to Jerusalem, to worship the Father. . . . The time is coming, nay, has already come, when true worshippers will worship the Father in spirit and in truth. . . ." (John iv. 21, 23). This announcement of Christ's was verified at the moment of his death, when the veil of the temple was rent, as a sign of the abolition of the worship held there; at the moment, too, of his resurrection, when his glorified body finally replaced the old temple; and, lastly, on the day of Pentecost, which was the completion of his Pasch. At the breath of the Spirit, there then occurred, through the dispersion of the apostolic preaching throughout the world, a kind of bursting asunder of Jerusalem. From then on the temple of God would be wherever there were worshippers in spirit and truth, in other words men who, receiving in faith the apostolic message, had become members of the Body of Christ. That is the law of Christian universality.

In space

All this is signified by the miracle of the speaking with tongues. This miracle has, doubtless, many different meanings, whether we take it as the apostles themselves speaking various languages, or as the various hearers each receiving the message in their own languages—the two interpretations are still disputed. It forms one of the elements of the Church's public character which is an essential feature of her coming into the world at Pentecost. Some commentators interpret it as a sign given specially to the Jews that, on account of their disbelief, the divine mission is to turn to the Gentiles. In any case, the universalist meaning is not to be lessened. At Pentecost there is proclaimed the Church's vocation to speak all tongues, to restore in Christ, in the Holy Ghost, the unity broken at Babel by the confusion of tongues.

This correspondence of Pentecost and Babel is often alluded to by the Fathers; and it has even been remarked, with some ingenuity, that the same word which, in the account of Babel, is used for dispersion, in the account of Pentecost expresses the division of the tongues of fire before settling on the heads of the apostles. This correspondence it is important to keep before our minds; for it makes clear one of the most essential aspects of the mystery of the Holy Ghost and of the Church, namely the reconstitution in God of the unity of the human family impaired, and more or less destroyed, by sin. The Fathers laid special stress on this, even though, in their day, the Roman Empire already held gathered into its unity so many different peoples, made one by their membership of the Catholic Church.

Do we really share their conviction on this ? Are we conscious of the reality of that great oneness of mind which is coextensive with the world, even goes beyond it, since it unites us with the dead, with the saints in heaven ? At this time, when the impulse to work, pray and suffer for Christian unity is felt by so many through the strong and gentle action of the Holy Ghost, we should remind ourselves that it is he who is able to bring back to unity souls so widely separated, not forcing them, but moving them from within so that the action seems wholly theirs. He brings about the fulfilment of the prayer "*Ut sint unum*—that all may be one". We, in our pilgrimage, keep before us an oecumenical intention, praying and hoping for the unity of all Christ's followers. (On the miracle of tongues, see de Lubac's *Catholicism*, chapter 2.)

In time

Universality in the geographical sense is not the only kind we have to speak of. We have to view at a deeper level the pentecostal force animating the apostolate or missionary activity. The mission, and the Church on earth itself, belongs essentially to the period between the first and second coming of Christ; for the essential message it delivers concerning Christ is that he who always was has come and will return (cf. Apoc. i. 4; iv. 8). At his first coming, which ended with his Pasch, Christ placed in the world a seed of universal salvation. The grain of wheat was placed in the earth, in solitude, and died there, but for the purpose of bringing forth much fruit. In his second coming, at the end of time, he will reap the harvest, separate the wheat from the chaff and gather it into his Father's house, where he has prepared us a place.

The apostolate or the mission, the Church in its entirety, all represent man's collaboration with God in bringing the grain of wheat placed in the earth by Christ's Pasch to the harvest of the Parousia. The dynamism for this is the Holy Spirit. Pentecost is for the sake of the whole world, to renew the face of the earth (Psalm ciii. 20 in the liturgy of the feast). But if Christ's work needs the Holy Spirit for it to reach the inmost heart of men, the Spirit of Pentecost, in turn, needs apostles for his breath to touch men. Through this collaboration, this "co-celebration", of the Holy Ghost and our apostolate, which together fill up the period between the two comings of Christ, the dynamism of God's plan of salvation is continually drawing on the treasure of grace and truth laid up by the Incarnation and the Pasch for the benefit of mankind. It applies these resources throughout the whole breadth of space and time, of the world and of history, to the human race ever working and expanding, that race which, placed in the world in the image of the first Adam, is to be raised to heaven in the image of the second Adam, Jesus Christ.

The Holy Ghost is the real soul, the divinely efficacious source of this movement. That is why, first of all, he "spoke by the prophets", who made known the plan of God's grace and proclaimed Christ. He speaks, likewise, by the apostles, by Stephen, Philip (Acts viii), by witnesses in every age, through all the various circumstances whose purpose he knows and directs. But throughout history Satan, also, the contradictor, the adversary (which is what the name means, transposed from the Hebrew), frustrates, as far as he can, the realization of the Kingdom and Plan of God, the dynamism of the Holy Spirit and the workings of the apostolate. What is going on today in the world in many different ways is a continuation of that resistance to God of which St. John speaks, which he made one of the basic themes of his gospel and first epistle. It is what we see all through the Acts and is denounced by Stephen, by St. Paul: "You resist the Holy Spirit" (vii. 51).

For this reason, the apostolate is always a call to conversion, to repentance, and the first act of the Holy Ghost is to convince the world of its wrong, of its sin (John xvi. 8 sq.). That, too, is why the apostle suffers from those afflictions inseparable from his messianic calling, inherent in the furtherance of the Kingdom of

God according to the purpose of his grace—Christ foretold it (Matthew x. 16 sq., note v. 20; John xv. 18), and St. Paul tells of its positive and joyful side (Coll. i. 24 sq.). That is why true witnesses are persecuted and put to death, why the Holy Ghost first sanctifies them by the Word and then gives them power. The dynamism of the apostolate comes wholly from the breath which Christ, dying on the cross, sent forth on Mary and John, who, at the foot of the cross, represented the Church, that is to say us (John xix. 30).

All Christian life is apostolic

It is easy to see how all Christian life should be, in one way or another, apostolic, since it is all vivified by this breath, it all derives from the Pasch and from Pentecost. For, ultimately, believing, loving, witnessing, praying, being an apostle, all come to the same thing. Prayer is to ask "thy kingdom come, thy will be done on earth as it is in heaven" and, since we cannot co-operate for this end except by the power of the Holy Ghost, "Give us this day our daily bread", the bread of faith and love, the bread of the mystical body.

"The seed is the word of God" (Mt. xiii; Mark iv; Luke 8), and the field is the whole world; not only the small land of Palestine, not only the Roman Empire, traversed in part by St. Paul, but the entire world, the world of all times, the world of today with its problems, its complexities, its immense ramifications in the matter of classes and races and all those new spheres constantly being opened up to the mind with bewildering rapidity. The harvest at hand is great, but there is a terrible dearth of labourers (Luke x. 2; cf. John iv. 34 sq.). The Fathers were fond of recalling that Pentecost represented in the Mosaic calendar the feast of the beginning of the harvest, of the first gathering of the sheaves. Christ, they said, gave the first stroke of the scythe and brought up to heaven the first sheaf, that of his body. The harvest has begun, it is to continue to the end of the field and until evening through the joint working of the Spirit and the apostolate. The Spirit will not be wanting; will apostles ever fail?

My fellow-pilgrims, I will make known to you a hope of mine. When a prisoner of war, I got to know of the construction of a way out of the camp which had been finally completed by the actual escape of a fellow-prisoner. What the ceremony proclaimed was effected. What will be the outcome of our observances today? We have talked and sung a great deal and prayed much in this atmosphere, at once serious and relaxed, of the journey to Chartres. Some of us will receive Confirmation, setting us on the line or the path which runs from Pentecost. We will sing, in the cathedral, of our joy at belonging to Christ, who has sent his Spirit into our hearts. Now what I hope is that all this will be followed by the departure to the missions of someone, man or woman, of our number, that the breath of the Lord will have that impulsive force.

Is that an idle hope ? There are many ways of going off to the work of the missions, and as many different calls of Our Lord. Anyhow, I confide my hope to Our Lady of Chartres.

APPENDIX

Passages bearing on the Holy Ghost and the Church

(1) From H. B. Swete, *The Holy Catholic Church*, Macmillan, 1919.

The communion of the Holy Spirit is not to be identified with our fellowship with Christ, although the former is inseparable from the latter. The Son was sent into the world, the spirit into the heart (Gal. lv. 4–6). The fellowship of the Spirit with the human spirit is immediate and direct. He who searches the deep things of God (1 Cor. ii. 10 sq.) enters also into the depths of our inner man. Our bodies become his shrine (1 Cor. vi. 19; cf. ii. 10), but his presence is out of sight, in the *penetralia* of our spirits, where he throws his searchlight on our unspoken thoughts and desires. His purpose is to carry forward the work of the divine philanthropy begun in the Incarnation, to make it bear on the centre of our being, regenerating and renewing the springs of our life (Titus iii. 4–6), changing our thoughts, shedding abroad within us the love of God, helping our infirmity, making intercession for the saints according to the will of God, sanctifying our whole nature in spirit, soul and body (Rom. viii. 5 sq.; viii. 26 sq.; 1 Thess. v. 25). But this work of sanctification is not a mechanical process, or an automatic growth; it is the result of the interaction of the divine and human in the inner life of men. . . .

There may indeed be conditions under which the action of the Divine Spirit can be distinctly recognized and his voice heard within. "The Spirit itself", St. Paul says, "beareth joint witness with our spirit, that we are children of God" (Rom. viii. 16, cf. ix. 1); together with the faltering, uncertain testimony of our own consciousness there may be heard from time to time a witness which we know to be divine. But ordinarily the fellowship is so close, the identification so complete, that the result may be attributed with equal correctness to ourselves, as led by the spirit, or to the Spirit who leads. Thus St. Paul can speak indifferently of "the Spirit of adoption whereby we cry, Abba, Father", and of the Spirit as himself uttering the same filial cry within our hearts (Rom. viii. 15; Gal. iv. 6). The cry is His, and it is ours: His cry in us, and ours in Him.

Thus the communion of the Holy Spirit—our fellowship with Him and His with us—is the normal condition of the Christian life, without which there can be no life in Christ which is worthy of the name (Rom. viii. 9). It is also a fact of Christian experience, although from the nature of the Spirit's operations they cannot usually be distinguished from the thoughts, affections, desires and actions which He prompts and energises. No Christian will fail to acknowledge that whatever is good in him is not of himself, but of the Holy Spirit. This is, in fact, to recognize that the Holy Spirit is at work at the springs of this new life; that he owes to fellowship with the Spirit the whole structure of the new self which is rising up within him—his faith, his love, his hope of eternal life. There would be no communion of saints in the Church of Christ—there would be no true saints to maintain communion with one another—if the Church had no Spirit of holiness, or no communion with Him. There could be no fellowship with the Father or with his Son Jesus Christ, if there were no fellowship of the Holy Spirit. Through the Son we all, Jewish and Gentile believers alike, have our access in one Spirit unto the Father (Eph. ii. 18).

(2) From J. A. Moehler, *Symbolism*, sec. 38.

After the divine Master had ascended into Heaven, when the time was fulfilled, the Holy Spirit came down on the apostles and disciples who had received the word of life. When they received light and strength from above, the heads and members of the Church just born were not found scattered in various places, but joined together in one place and in one heart, being a single gathering of brethren; they had, in fact, been formally commanded to wait in Jerusalem for the Paraclete.

Further, the divine Spirit took an outward form of tongues of fire, a symbol of his strength which purifies men's hearts from all evil and reunites them in love. He did not will to come in a purely interior way, as if to seal and consecrate an invisible society; but, just as the Word had been made flesh, the Spirit also came in a way perceptible to the senses, to the accompaniment of a loud noise like a mighty wind.

Thus each disciple was filled with heavenly gifts only because he formed a moral unity with all the rest; and the divine Spirit came down from heaven and imparted his graces only under sensible forms.

In the same way, by Christ's institution, the union of man with God can be wrought only under certain exterior forms and in the fellowship of the faithful. As to exterior forms, what are the sacraments but sensible signs of the spiritual gifts attached to them! In the fellowship of the faithful, since no one can baptise himself, and all are sent to those who are already members of the Church. Once the neophyte has entered into the fellowship of the children of God, he has to attach himself to it ever more closely. Baptism, the gateway into the heavenly fold, gives him the right, or rather imposes the duty, to share in all the joys and all the sorrows of the community. At the same time, the administration of the sacraments, as well as that of the word, has been entrusted by the Lord to the apostolate; and in this respect, too, the faithful are closely incorporated with the community, bound to it indissolubly. So then, union with Christ implies union with his Church. The bonds joining men with Christ bind them to the Church; the two are inseparable, he is in her and she in him (Eph. v. 29–32).

For these same reasons, the Church cannot fail in that part of her mission which is to preserve in its purity the word of God; she is not liable to error. As each one who worships Christ is necessarily incorporated in the Church; as he is brought to Christ through her, and remains in Christ only in so far as he dwells in her, it is the Church, too, who forms his heart and mind. He cannot then refuse her his confidence. It follows that this confidence should be deserved, and that the believer who abandons himself into the hands of the Church cannot be led into error. Consequently, the Church is infallible.

Infallibility, however, does not belong to any individual as such. Since he is a part of an organic whole, the individual Christian is protected from deception only by thinking and willing in the mind and heart of all. To conceive otherwise the relations of the members with the body would be to deprive the Church of any foundation; for, if this divine community is necessary, that is because the union of all is the first condition of the Christian life, and isolation is the death of any real faith and solid piety.

So it is that the Catholic has for the Church a profound respect, unutterable love, boundless submission. The idea of resisting, of rebelling against, her is repugnant to him in his innermost being, to start a schism and break up her unity is a crime that fills him with horror and dread. The idea of community, on the other hand, warms the heart, appeals to the reason and corresponds admirably to all our religious and moral instincts.

(3) From Moehler, *Unity in the Church, or the principle of Catholicism, according to the Fathers of the first three centuries.*

Before the coming of Christ, the Spirit which formed, animated and held together in one body all those who believed, came down but rarely and only on individuals living widely apart. For that reason, there was no possibility of a common religious and spiritual life; what life there was showed itself only sporadic and exceptional manifestations. It was only after the spectacular and miraculous descent of this same spirit of God on the apostles and on the whole Christian community that this latter began to live truly as such. From that time the Spirit was never to leave the believers; he had not to return, since he was eternally present. The aggregate of all the faithful, that is to say the Church, has now become, through the presence in it of the Holy Spirit, the inexhaustible treasure, the source ever flowing, the youth always renewing itself, the new principle of life, and offers to all an abundant sustenance.

St. Irenaeus says: "We keep intact the faith received by the Church, because it is a gift of the Holy Spirit. This faith might be likened to a precious jewel in a fine case, if these were capable of ever renewing their youth. God has entrusted to the Church the mission of distributing his Spirit to his human creatures, so that all the members receiving it may be vivified. That is the essence of our bond with Christ; it is there that is manifested the power of the Holy Spirit. It is the Holy Spirit that is the pledge of the perennial duration of our faith, of its growth and development in us; the Spirit is the way leading us to God. Where the Church is, there also is the Spirit of God. There the Spirit of God is, there also is the Church and the fullness of grace. The Spirit is truth. For that reason, those who seek the food of their souls outside the maternal bosom of the Church have no part in Christ, and do not receive the living and pure waters which flow like a torrent from the mystical body" (*Adv. Haer.* iii. 24, 1; P.G., 7966).

St. Cyprian says the same: "The Church, penetrated by the

light of the Lord, spreads abroad its rays through the entire world. This light is scattered in all parts, while yet the unity of the body remains perfect . . ." (*De unitate*, 5).

II

The Church and Its Unity

I

THE CHURCH is the realization of the New Covenant, the community of those who, reconciled with God in Christ's death and resurrection, are called to live with God as his sons, citizens of the heavenly city, and to enter on a share in the inheritance of God. The mystery of the Church was already in part realized and made known in the Old Testament by the formation of a people of God. This began with God's promises to Abraham, and the alliance entered into with him and his descendants (Gen. xii. 2, 3 and 7; xiii. 14–17; xv. 1 sq.; xviii. 1–8). Abraham was promised an inheritance and an heir. The heir was a son born to him of Sarah and, after him, a whole succession, a race which, as God disclosed to Abraham, would become as numerous as the stars of heaven. The inheritance was the land of Chanaan, which God assigned, as if by testament, to Abraham and his race (1 Kings viii. 36; cf. Deut. i. 8). This land was, as it were, an inheritance received from God by Abraham and his posterity, and the fruit of the alliance (Gen. xv. 18 sq.) of which circumcision was the sign (Gen. xvii. 9 sq.).

The alliance was renewed between God and Moses as representing Abraham's posterity, now the people of Israel, on Sinai (Ex. xix. 1–6). This time, it was given a precise basis, namely the law God gave to his people by whose observance Israel was to be truly the people of God (Ex. xx.; xxiv. 7–8, 27; cf. Heb. ix. 20). Such, in fact, were the terms of the alliance; it was an interchange of mutual fidelity and, so to speak, of property, expressed by the prophets under the forceful simile of a marriage between Israel and Jahve. Israel was to be the one people of God among all the peoples of the earth, which means it would observe with unremitting zeal and the most delicate fidelity Jahve's will and commandments. In return, Jahve, the God of the whole earth, would be, in special fashion, the God of Israel, his people; he would protect them and be always with them against their enemies, the common enemies of both. Further, over and above this pledge of mutual fidelity, there opens up a prospect rich in values of the religious sphere. By its fidelity to Jahve and observance of his will, Israel is to become itself something religious and sacred, raised up, as it were, to the sphere of the divine life. The alliance establishes, between the people and God, a sort of bond of mystical relationship; Jahve dwells in Israel (Lev. xxvi. 12; Ez. xxxvii. 27; Is. lx), he is *its* God. Israel, for its part, is the people *of God*, his kingdom, his portion, his heritage, his property, his vine. Living under divine rule, a theocratic nation, it is for God "a priestly kingdom and a holy nation" (Ex. xix. 6).

The promises made to Abraham, the alliance entered into with him and renewed with Moses and, later on, with David (promised an everlasting throne), are all concerned with a heritage that is "the earth", and an heir who is Israel, the posterity of Abraham.

The old alliance was made with a people understood in a racial and carnal sense, and the benefits received as a heritage from God were material and earthly. None the less, as a result of the preaching of the prophets and, particularly, when Israel was, through its own fault, deprived of "the land" and driven into exile, the ideas both of the people of God and its heritage became broadened and spiritualised. The heir was now not only the carnal people, the purely racial community, but an Israel taken in a wholly religious sense, a people consisting of the meek, the pious and the holy; the scope of God's summons extended beyond ethnical frontiers to include all men and peoples desirous of obeying God in justice (e.g. Isaias ii. 1 sq.; lvi, etc.). At the same time, the idea of the benefits of the alliance, the inheritance from God, became more definite and spiritual; from being merely "the land", it became a state of things where God would reign in justice. Submission to the yoke of his reign was necessary, and those who did so would themselves reign with God, would inherit his glory. The fulfilment of the promises, the entry on the true goods of the alliance, were now attached to a time yet to come, when, under the leadership of a King-Messias, full of wisdom, piety, and the spirit of Jahve (Isaias xi, etc.), Israel would become, among the nations, the instrument—and, at the same time, the privileged beneficiary—of the Kingdom of God.

Beyond even this kingdom of God to be set up on earth, a kingdom which a zealous, just and religious Israel was to inherit from God, there came a proclamation of an eternal kingdom in Daniel (ch. vii). Who were to be the beneficiaries of this? They are, at one and the same time, an individual being, coming "on the clouds, like to the Son of Man" (v. 13), to whom are given "power and glory and a kingdom" for eternity, and also "the people of the saints of the Most High", who receive equally "the kingdom and the power and the greatness of the kingdoms under the whole heaven" (v. 27). Here we already have, in a highly significant way, one of the features which will be dominant, even decisive, in the Christian idea of the Kingdom and of the Church—the real identity of an individual and a collectivity, all being in a single one, all belonging to a single one, and yet all being realized in a collectivity, all belonging to a people.

We may note, too, at this point, that St. Paul's idea of the mystical Body as the idea of a certain relationship between an individual and a group, has a Jewish background, and rests on the extremely vivid awareness, in the Old Testament, of the solidarity of the members of Israel with God. Israel is a people, a single blood ("those of my blood", says St. Paul). The religious consciousness of Israel and the call of each person are bound up with the destiny of the group, and this destiny is expressed, is summed up and, as it were, realized in the great religious personalities, the Fathers of Israel, in consideration of whom and in the person of whom God looks with favour on his people.

Finally, the old alliance, even in its most spiritualised form, is acknowledged to be superseded at a future time. Jeremias (xxxi. 31–34, cited in Heb. viii. 8–12), Ezechiel (xxxviii. 26–28), and, in particular, Zacharias (ii. 5 sq.; iii. 6–10; vi. 12 sq.; ix. 9 sq.) announce the conclusion of a new alliance. There will be a new order of things corresponding to the messianic era, which will be characterized, on the one hand, by the extension of Jahve's reign through Israel to the whole world and, on the other, by a new regime of wisdom, gentleness, peace, thanks to the sending down of the Spirit of God on the King-Messias and his people.

II

This is the new order whose realization is proclaimed by Our Lord, at the outset of his public ministry (Luke iv. 21, referring to Isaias lxi, 1 sq.), then by Peter at Pentecost (Acts ii. 16, referring to Joel iii. 1–5). The messianic era has come; it is also the "last times", the eschatological—not that the final catastrophe is necessarily at hand from the point of view of duration, but that mankind has now entered the final order of things, into a world which will have no successor, for it is the order of eternal life. This order may well be not yet perfect and, consequently, be awaiting its completion; but it is already inaugurated and set in being.

In this new order, the inheritance promised to Abraham and called "the land" is radically transformed. It is still an inheritance received from God; but what we are called to, the goods of which the people of the new alliance are to enter into possession, is no other than the patrimony of God himself. What the Alliance, the Blood of the New Testament, opens out to us is access to the heavenly inheritance (Heb. ix. 15; Col. iii. 24), an incorruptible inheritance (1 Peter i. 4), the inheritance of the kingdom (Eph.

v. 5; James ii. 5), of eternal life. It is access to Mount Sion, the city of the living God, which is the heavenly Jerusalem (Heb. xii. 22 sq.). We enter, by the new alliance, into the city of the saints (Eph. ii. 18–19; Phil. iii. 20), we have communion of life with God (Cor. i. 9; 1 John i. 3), we have eternal life (1 John v. 11–13).

But this wonderful transformation of our inheritance is perforce accompanied by an equally profound change in the person inheriting and in this way the promises made to Abraham are splendidly fulfilled. We can have part in the patrimony of God as an inheritance only in Christ. He alone is truly heir of God since he is, on the one hand, by nature Son of the Father and, on the other, a descendant of Abraham according to the flesh, the flesh he took from Mary. He is, therefore, at once the natural heir of all the Father's goods ("omnia mea tua sunt"—John xvii. 10) and heir, by descent, of the promises made to Abraham which are to be realized in him—"for in him all the promises of God become certain" (2 Cor. i. 20). We know how St. Paul, in his account of justification by faith, argues that the promises were made to Abraham and his seed, that is to say, to one, who is Christ (Gal. iii. 18, 29). Christ, heir by nature to the Father's goods, is also the true beneficiary of the original promises; but the inheritance which these referred to obscurely is now revealed as being that of the saints in light, the patrimony of the Father. We, too, enter into this inheritance, in Christ; we are co-heirs with him (Rom. viii. 14–17; Eph. iii. 6; Tit. iii. 7; 1 Peter iii. 22; 1 John iii. 1). In him we inherit both the promises made to Israel—for we are the new people of Israel, the new people of God—and the goods belonging to him as Son. In this way, Christ is the sole subject by right to whom belongs this heavenly inheritance, for "no man hath ascended into heaven, but he that descended from heaven, the Son of Man" (John iii. 13); but, if we become his members, we ascend there with him and, with him, we have access to the Father. In him we are able to lead the life of sons that we have received, the life of children in the family of God.

All this is the object of the faith and hope to which we have been called. St. Paul, who speaks mainly of the Redemption as completed, as involving the total transformation of man, the glorification of the body, total victory over sin and death—St. Paul, who had known the glorified Christ on the road to Damascus, speaks preferably of the future state of this inheritance of eternal life (Rom. v. 5; viii. 19, 23, 24; xiii. 11; 1 Cor. vi. 9–10; Eph. i. 14; v. 30; 2 Thess. ii. 11–14; 1 Tim. vi. 12, etc.) St. John, on the other hand, speaks more of the present—we already have eternal life (1 John iii. 1–2; v. 11 and 13); but he does not overlook that it still awaits fulfilment (1 John iii. 2), and St. Paul is fully aware that this life has already begun in us, since we live by Christ. The good things of the Kingdom are given us in a precarious, imperfect and hidden, but yet real, manner. He speaks of the first-fruits of the Spirit, by which he means, not any sort of a pledge, but a pledge which consists of a beginning, here and now, of what we wait for, in faith and hope.

Thus, we see a double element, among many others, in this New Testament revelation of what the mystery of the Church is both in the synoptics, where it is presented in terms of a Kingdom, and in St. John, who expresses it as a form of life, and in St. Paul, who speaks of it as the new creation, the restoration of all things in Christ and, finally, as his mystical Body. In all of these we find that (1) the city of God is wholly in a single individual and yet it is also a people, a multitude; (2) the city of God is already present and yet is to be consummated in the future. Since we are in the order of the new alliance, we are in that of the final and definitive realities; but these are given to us and are present in a restricted and precarious way, their full manifestation is yet to come.

These characteristics belong, also, to the sacraments which are signs of the Alliance brought about in Christ and refer to a threefold reality—to the past but ever active and efficacious reality of Christ's Passion, in which the reconciliation of us all and the whole world is already accomplished; to a present reality of grace, by which eternal life is given to us now and the mystical Body constituted; finally, to the future reality of the consummation in glory, which the sacrament proclaims and of which it is the pledge (cf. St. Thomas, *Summa Theol.* IIIa, 9. 60, a. 3 and q. 73, a. 4).

III

We will now turn to examine in what consists the present reality of this renewal brought about by Christ and, to begin with, in Christ himself.

All the promises made to Israel become, in fact, a reality in Christ. He is himself their fulfilment, the Alpha and Omega. The whole reality of the new creation is in him, and we become sharers in it only if we are "found in him". He has, indeed, realized the new alliance for us, not only by representing us before the Father as the chief man represents his people, but by containing us in himself as a living body contains its members. Further, this new alliance, made with the most holy God for sinners, lost and condemned to death, was concluded by him in his own blood offered in sacrifice for us. This most pure offering was declared efficacious by God raising up the victim of Calvary and his ascension into heaven, God thus testifying that access to him had become once more possible and that the heavcnly goods, his own patrimony in fact, had been gained by the blood of the new and eternal alliance. This sublime mystery is expressed by St. Paul in the most vigorous terms: "Now you are in Christ Jesus; now, through the blood of Christ, you have been brought close, you who were once so far away. He is our bond of peace; he has made the two nations one, breaking down the wall that was a barrier between us. He has put an end to the law with its decrees, so as to make peace, remaking the two human creatures as one in himself; both sides, united in a single body, he would reconcile to God through the cross, inflicting death, in his own person, upon the feud. . . . United in the same Spirit, we have access through him to the Father" (Eph. ii. 13–18). "If one man died on behalf of all, then all thereby became dead men; Christ died for us all, so that being alive should no longer mean living with our own life, but with his life who died for us and has risen again. . . . This, as always, is God's doing; it is he who through Christ has reconciled us to himself. . . . Yes, God was in Christ, reconciling the world to himself" (2 Cor. v. 14, 15, 18, 19). "It was God's good pleasure . . . through him to win back all things, whether on earth or in heaven, into union with himself, make peace with them through his blood shed on the cross" (Col. i. 20).

So we are reconciled with God in Christ because he has performed for us, containing us all in himself, those redemptive acts which constitute the one and threefold mystery of his passion-resurrection-ascension—a single mystery, which St. John calls that of the "passing of Christ to his Father", and which Our Lord, in the same Gospel, calls his glorification; redemptive acts wherein Christ truly fulfils his function of Christ and Head[1] in which he acts wholly for us, for the new Israel thereby made sharers in the good things of the alliance he established. It was then that our salvation was secured, in him who was "delivered up for our sins and risen for our justification".[2] All that is needed is for us to make effectual, in our own regard, the mystery accomplished for our sakes, to associate ourselves with Christ in his passing to the Father, in order to become, in him, sharers in the good things of God, to be, in the well-known words of St. Paul, "associated in his death", "associated in his resurrection", so as to be "associated with him in glory" and "associated with him in his place in heaven"[3].

If he is thus our peace (Eph. ii. 14; cf. Isaias xlii. 6), if we have

[1] So it is that the apostles said, quite simply, that the resurrection declared Christ to be Son of God and made him Lord (Acts ii. 36; Rom. i. 3–4; cf. Phil. ii. 7–11, etc.).

[2] Rom. iv. 25. This idea is brought out strongly and excellently related to the mystery of the Church in its entirety in Ramsay's *The Gospel and the Catholic Church*, London, 1936.

[3] These are the famous verbs compounded of συν, on which see, especially Prat's Theology of St. Paul, vol. ii; or, indeed, any work on Pauline theology.

in him redemption, wisdom, justice, sanctification and all things (1 Cor. i. 30; Eph. i. 7 sq.), if we are reconciled with God in him, this is all because he is the head, the principle of the entire new order of things he has initiated. St. Paul expresses this; in two ways, by the idea of "head",[1] and that of the "second Adam":[2] "A man had brought us death, and a man should bring us resurrection from the dead; just as all have died with Adam, so with Christ all will be brought to life. . . . Mankind begins with the Adam who became, as Scripture tells us, a living soul; it is fulfilled in the Adam who has become a life-giving spirit. . . . The man who first came from earth, fashioned of dust, the man who afterwards came from heaven, and his fashion is heavenly. The nature of that earth-born man is shared by his earthly sons, the nature of the heaven-born man, by his heavenly sons; and it remains for us, who once bore the stamp of earth, to bear the stamp of heaven. What I mean, brethren, is this: the kingdom of God cannot be enjoyed by flesh and blood; the principle of corruption cannot share a life which is incorruptible" (1 Cor. xv. 21–22, 45–50; cf. Rom. v. 14). We may note, in passing, the perfect equivalence of the two realities, namely the new order of which Christ, the second Adam, is the source, and the kingdom we are to inherit. Christ is, as Head, the source of a new life, of a new being, for the whole of creation—"when a man becomes a new creature in Christ, his old life has disappeared" (2 Cor. v. 17). As second Adam, he is the source of a renewal which makes new men of all who are "in Christ Jesus" (Eph. ii. 10); as the first Adam is, for mankind, the source of a "psychic" life, a carnal life, the second Adam is, for man regenerated, the source of a "pneumatic" life, of a life holy and heavenly. He became such, we have said, on the cross, by the one means of his passion-resurrection-ascension. Thus, the Fathers and the writers of the

[1] In the two Epistles, Ephesians and Colossians, where he is concerned to assert the unique sovereignty of Christ against a kind of gnosticism which worshipped spirits. Cf. Eph., I, 22–23; Iv, 15–16; V, 22 ff.; Col., I, 18; II, 10 and 19.

2. See Prat, op. cit.

Middle Ages saw profoundly into the nature of the Church when they represented it as coming out from the side of Christ on the cross, symbolized by the water and blood which themselves represent the sacraments of Baptism and the Eucharist. Just as, so they assert, Eve was made from the side of Adam in his sleep, so the Church came out from the side of Christ on the cross, in the sleep of death;[1] and again, "ex latere dormientis in cruce sacramenta profluxerunt, quibus Ecclesia fabricatur".[2]

Finally, if Christ is, both as second Adam and as Head, the source of the new order of things which is the Church, that is because he possesses in himself the fullness of the divine being and power. St. Paul tells us expressly that, if he is Head, it is because he is the *pleroma*—"He is the Head whose body is the Church; it begins with him, since his was the first birth out of death; thus in every way the primacy was to become his. For it was God's good pleasure to let all completeness dwell in him . . ." (Col. i. 18–19). It is because the fullness of the divine being and activity dwells in Christ that he is, for mankind and the whole creation a source of renewal and of communication of divine life (cf. Eph. i. 23; iii. 19; iv. 12 sq.; Col. ii. 9 sq.). Thus, all things, since they are gathered under Christ as head and receive from him, as a body from its head, a new life, are taken up into Christ, "recapitulated" in him—"it was his loving design, centred in Christ, to give history its fulfilment by resuming everything in him, all that is in heaven, all that is on earth, summed up in him" (Eph. i. 9–10). In Christ the fullness of life is, indeed, restored and the result of this restoration, as brought about in space and time, is simply the Church. Consequently, the Church is presented to us as from the very beginning essentially catholic, that is to say embracing the whole universe of being and of beings in unity, catholic by reason of a catholicity it derives from

1 The same idea is expressed in the theology and iconography of the tree of life, and later, of the mystical fountain of the sacraments.

2 Cf., among the numerous texts in this connection, St. Thomas, *iv Sent.*, d. 18, q. 1, a. 1, sol. 1; St. Bonaventure, *ii Sent.*, d. 18, a. 1, q. 1, resp.

its source, Christ, in whom dwells the fullness of the divine energy capable of reconciling, purifying, unifying and transfiguring the world.

This catholicity involves unity and holiness for the three have, fundamentally, the same reality for their source. The Church is one because Christ is one of whom it is the body; it is holy because the being Christ gives it is something holy, something heavenly, "pneumatic"; it is Catholic, because its head has the power to communicate it a life and a force capable of reuniting through its means, in him, all things, those in heaven and those on earth.

So we arrive at the existence of One, Holy, Catholic Church, the Jerusalem which is above and below at the same time, the City of the Saints being built up amongst men, to which access is opened up to us by the blood of the New Testament.

IV

This Church is, in the first place, the Body of Christ; it forms, with him, a single entity, a single beneficiary of the good things of God—"the Gentiles are to win the same inheritance, to be made part of the same body, to share the same divine promise, in Christ Jesus" (Eph. iii. 6). We are with Christ a single body, we are members of this body (Rom. xii. 3 sq.; Eph. iv. 13 and 25 sq.; Col. iii. 15 sq.). St. Paul goes so far as to say that we are a single person in Christ (Gal. iii. 28). We must now examine this reality of Christ in us, of the mystical Body, of the renewal effected by Christ in us.

How does this all come about? St. Paul makes it abundantly clear; on the one hand, "mankind begins with the Adam who became a living soul; it is fulfilled in the Adam who has become a life-giving spirit" (1 Cor. xv. 45), on the other, "a man's body is all one, though it has a number of different organs; and all this multitude of organs goes to make up one body; so it is with Christ. We too, all of us, have been baptized into a single body by the power of a single Spirit, Jews and Greeks, slaves and free men alike; we have all been given to drink at a single source, the one Spirit" (1 Cor. xii. 12–13). What brings it about that there is a single body in Christ is that animating this body is a single spirit, the Spirit of Christ. We have already seen that the time of the Messias was characterized, in the Old Testament, by a pouring out of the Spirit of God, which would fill the Messias himself, in the first place. Christ, risen and glorified, is able to give his Spirit. After having brought about in himself, for us, peace with God in the threefold and single mystery of his passion-resurrection-ascension, he has now gone up to heaven "to fill creation with his presence" (Eph. iv. 10). What he has accomplished in himself for our salvation he will now do in us for his glory. Now that he has become *Kyrios* and life-giving spirit, he is immanent in his body by his spirit. The Ascension is followed by Pentecost; the Church he founded in himself by the Passion undergone for us he now founds in us and in the world by the sending forth of his Spirit. So then, whatever Christ does as regards the setting up of the Church, his Body, whether in each of us individually or in the life of the whole, is, from now on, attributed equally to his Spirit. This Spirit it is, the "other Paraclete", who is Christ's agent in his Church and the book of the Acts may well be called the Gospel of the Holy Spirit. All that St. Paul attributes to Christ in the life of the Christian he attributes equally, in almost the same terms, to the Holy Spirit.

This immanence of the living Christ in the Church, his Body, is expressed by St. Paul in two very familiar phrases, each of which, ultimately, indicates the same thing—Christ in us, and we in Christ. The formula, "in Christ Jesus", which, counting equivalent expressions, occurs one hundred and forty-four times, signifies being under his influence, receiving life and movement from him and, consequently, acting, as it were, on his account through performing actions that are really his and belong to the sphere which he animates; it amounts to saying, "in his body". The corresponding formula, "Christ in us", signifies his being in us as our life, as an interior principle of action; it expresses the basis of all the Pauline mysticism of the Christian life as consisting in the imitation of Christ, in having in oneself the sentiments of Christ, the mind of Christ (1 Cor. ii. 16), and in Christ being formed in us (Gal. iv. 19). The two formulas express basically the same reality; what the Christian does as a Christian is an act of Christ, since the Christian is a member of Christ. Christians altogether, animated by the same spirit and acting in the name and under the impulse of the same Lord, form a single whole, the Body of Christ. For, as the body is animated by the soul, which it makes visible and expresses in all kinds of actions, so the Church is animated by Christ, makes him visible and expresses him in its various activities. In one sense, it adds nothing to Christ; it is simply his visibility in extended and tangible form, the visible body of his Spirit, of his Πνεῦμα.[1] In another, it adds something to him; it is his fulness and, in realizing itself, realizes Christ, till "we shall reach . . . that maturity which is proportioned to the completed growth of Christ" (Eph. iv. 13).[2]

In this way, the mystery of the mystical Body, like that of the Kingdom, brings us in contact with a twofold and antithetical truth. Everything is already fulfilled in Christ; the Church is simply the manifestation of what is in him, the visible reality animated by his Spirit. Yet, we have still to realize Christ and build up his body. This twofold truth we would call a *dialectic* of the "datum" and the "agi"; it is closely bound up with the mystery of the theandric reality of the Church, and we meet it also in connection with the sacraments.

If we go on to inquire what part we are called to contribute to the building up of the mystical Body, we shall have to speak, along with St. Paul, of faith and charity, and, from that, of the

[1] St. Paul and the Fathers up to the 10th or 11th century speak simply of the "body of Christ". The adjective "mystical", brought in by way of distinction from the eucharistic body, signifying "spiritual", "pneumatic", distinguished the Church as Body of Christ from the physical reality of "Christ accordingto the flesh".

[2] Cf. Col. i. 24: "I help to pay off the debt which the afflictions of Christ leave still to be paid, for the sake of his Body, the Church". There is, likewise, the modern idea that we are a kind of "additional human nature" for Christ (*humanité de surcroit*—Gay), but this is only a derivative from St. Paul's teaching.

whole moral life considered as a *vita in Christo*. There is such an abundance of texts in this connection that we should have to cite practically the whole of St. Paul, and to follow it with considerable extracts from the epistles of St. Peter and St. John. We will just give two, as being the most comprehensive. "May Christ find a dwelling-place, through faith, in your hearts; may your lives be rooted in love, founded on love" (Eph. iii. 17); ". . . build up the frame of Christ's body, until we all realize our common unity through faith. . . . We are to follow the truth in a spirit of charity, and so grow up, in everything, into a due proportion with Christ, who is our head. On him all the body depends; it is organized and unified by each contact with the source which supplies it, and thus, each limb receiving the active power it needs, it achieves its natural growth, building itself up through charity" (Eph. iv. 12–16).

Later on, we shall show[1] how faith and charity, faith animated by charity and bearing fruit in good works (Gal. v. 6), bring about the realization of the mystical Body, by realizing the "Christ in us" and the "we in Christ". For it is faith that opens up our soul to the point of view of another and causes his way of seeing things to come alive in us; and it is charity that makes us embrace and adopt his ideas and propensities, his motives of conduct. Supernatural faith is, so to speak, Christ's vision engrafted on us, and charity his heart living in the place of our own. By faith and charity, our life is given over to Christ, it becomes in reality a life on his account—"I am alive; or rather, not I it is Christ that lives in me. True, I am living, here and now, this mortal life; but my real life is the faith I have in the Son of God, who loved me, and gave himself for me" (Gal. ii. 20). This explains a passage from

[1] There are a number of passages in the theologians which make living faith the very substance of the mystical body. "Incorporamur Christo per fidem et caritatem", says St. Thomas, *Summa Theol.*, pars. iii, q. 80, a. 2, c., ad. 3, and a. 4; iv *Sent.*, d. 9, q. 1, a. 2, sol. 4; *Com. in Joann.*, c. vii, lect. 7, n. 2, 3, 4 and 6. Cf. *Com. in Gal.*, c. vi, lect. 4: "Fides caritate formata est nova creatura. . . . Sic ergo per novam creaturam, scilicet per fidem Christi et caritatem Dei, quae diffusa est in cordibus nostris, renovamur, et Christo conjungimur".

the martyr, St. Ignatius, which many a critic has objected to: "Faith, which is the Lord's flesh, and charity, which is his blood" (*Ad Trall.* viii, 1). By faith, we are truly members of Christ and, by charity, his living members. We make Christ live in us, and we live in him; we lead a life on his account and under his vital impulse.

Faith and charity set in motion and inform all the other virtues. They are the springs of the whole life of the Christian and, through them, all his actions, sentiments and thoughts are effected in Christ. By letting all his actions be animated by a living faith, all he does will be done in Christ. His friends will be friends in Christ, his work will be done in Christ; whatever it may be, he will bring Christ into it, by a living faith, through charity, prayer and grace. He is sad in Christ, ill in Christ, kind and devoted in Christ, chaste, patient and mortified in Christ. So with everything, with the result that whatever in us derives from the first Adam and is animated by a "psychic" life becomes life in the second Adam, becomes part of our life in Christ or of Christ in us. The whole, then, is recapitulated in Christ until, with everything brought into subjection to him, the Son himself pays homage to him who has subjected all to him, so that God may be all in all (cf. Eph. i. 10; 1 Cor. xv. 28; Col. iii. 11).

In this way, the body of the second Adam is formed, by the gradual communication of his Spirit to all that is material, to the whole range of human actions that proceed throughout the world from the increasing progeny of the first Adam. There can be no question of separating Christianity from mankind's various activities, professional, social, cultural. Doubtless, there is often, in practice, opposition between the carnal man and the spiritual and all our natural activities proceed from a "body of sin" (Rom. vi. 6). But St. Paul summons us to "mortify the ways of nature through the power of the Spirit" (Rom. viii. 13), to "live by the Spirit" (Gal. v. 25)[1], and to "offer up your bodies as

[1] Gal. v. 22–24: The 'Fruits of the Spirit' would seem to represent the very substance of the kingdom and the new creation.

a living sacrifice, consecrated to God and worthy of his acceptance" (Rom. xii. 1; cf. vi. 13 and 1 Cor. vi. 15–17).

In this regard, the idea of the mystical Body scts before us a highly realistic view. It makes us see how Christ wills to continue his life in men, in a truly theandric way. He wills to continue in us what he first did for us. He wishes to be a child in the Christian child, obedient in its obedience, to lead a family life in Christian homes and married people, to be joyful in those who rejoice, to continue his Passion in those who suffer (Col. i. 24), to teach in the Christian teacher, to work in the Christian worker, in short, to animate in us every living fibre of mankind, so as to "recapitulate" all in him.

Of all this, the first Christian generations had a very lively sense. In his excellent study on the Church, *Der Quellort*, F. Kattenbusch shows how they looked on the Church as something come down from heaven to earth, the heavenly world being, essentially, that of the Spirit and of holiness. Besides being a gift from above, the coming to us of the heavenly Jerusalem from the side of God (Apoc. xxi. 2 sq.), the Church was, for them, essentially, the *Agape*, a community where all helped one another freely and spontaneously. Thus, it was, in accordance with the dialectic of the "datum" and the "agi", both a gift of God sent from above, and the effect of the co-operation of men, a reality given and an active realization, mystical Body and community.

V

All through the writings of the apostolic age and the earliest period of Christianity, we see treated as identical, without the slightest separation of the two, the community life in Christ and the mystical Body, on the one hand, and the actual community of Christians, on the other.

One thing of incalculable importance, though somewhat ignored for the past forty years, has been brought to the fore in some recent works[1], namely, that the constitution of the mystical

[1] Protestant, especially such as those of Schweitzer in Germany, and Goguel in France.

Body and the realization of its unity are, in St. Paul, dependent on a sacramental action. Faith is the ground on which we are justified and we grow as members of Christ through acts that are animated by a living faith; but it is Baptism that incorporates us in him, and the Eucharist that makes us all a single body, his body. The texts are well known but it is essential at this point, to recall them.

BAPTISM. "We, all of us, have been baptised into a single body by the power of a single Spirit, Jews and Greeks, slaves and free men alike; we have all been given drink at a single source, the one Spirit" (1 Cor. xxi. 13). "All you who have been baptised in Christ have put on the person of Christ; no more Jew or Gentile, no more slave and freeman, no more male and female; you are all one person in Christ. And if you belong to Christ, then you are indeed Abraham's children; the promised inheritance is yours" (Gal. iii. 26–29).

Baptism makes us put on Christ, that is, to enter under the influence of his Spirit; it makes us one body with him, because it animates us with his Spirit. Consequently, it is at Baptism and through Baptism that takes place the mystery of the passing from the first Adam to the second, from the "psychic" to the "pneumatic" mode of animation. How does this happen? Because the sacramental act (always presupposing faith) puts at our actual disposition the redemptive mystery accomplished by Christ in his flesh for us. In the sacramental celebration, real and symbolic at the same time, of a mystery the meaning of whose rite is given by faith (*sacramenta fidei*), there is effectively produced our death with Christ, as beings carnal and "psychic", and our reanimation by his Spirit, inaugurating a "life for God" (Rom. vi. 10); hence the magnificent symbolism of Baptism explained by St. Paul in his epistles to the Romans (vi. 1–11) and to the Colossians (ii. 9–12). Thus Baptism brings about, by its own sole agency, the substance of Christianity, since it gives a real share in the mystery of Christ's redemption and animates the soul in view of eternal life. So it is not to be wondered at that St. Paul makes it the very foundation of our right to the inheritance of eternal life—"He saved us with the cleansing power that gives us new birth, and restores our nature through the Holy Spirit, shed on us in abundant measure through our Saviour, Jesus Christ. So, justified by his grace, we were to become heirs, with the hope of eternal life set before us" (Titus iii. 5–7).[1] This doctrine of St. Paul's is no different from that of the Synoptics—"He that believes and is baptised shall be saved" (Mark xvi. 16; cf. Mt. xxviii. 19)—and of St. John—"A man cannot see the kingdom of God without being born anew. No man can enter into the kingdom of God unless birth comes to him from water and from the Holy Spirit. What is born by natural birth is a thing of nature, what is born by spiritual birth is a thing of spirit" (iii. 3, 5 and 6).

THE EUCHARIST. "We have a cup that we bless; is not this cup we bless a participation in Christ's blood? Is not the bread we break a participation in Christ's body? The one bread makes us one body, though we are many in number; the same bread is shared by all" (1 Cor. x. 16–17). Baptism links us up with the redemptive mystery of the Passion and Resurrection; it joins us to the body of Christ, making us members of a body at peace and union with God. The Eucharist makes us live accordingly. As a sacramental action performed in memory of the Passion, a communion with the blood of the New Testament, it gives us as food the bread delivered up for the salvation of the world, which itself gives eternal life (John vi. 51). By its means, Christ's life takes possession of us, somewhat as, in the Trinity, the life of the Father fills and penetrates the Son (John vi. 57). In this way, the Eucharist brings to pass the whole scheme outlined by St. Paul and St. John, the Son having in himself the fullness of the Godhead and living by the Father, and each Christian having in himself the life of Christ and living by him. St. John then rightly attributes to the Eucharist the fact of the Christian being in Christ and Christ in the Christian, which St. Paul sees as the charac-

[1] Cf. Gal. iii. 29 and Col. i. 13, which many commentators apply to Baptism.

teristic of the mystical Body (John vi. 54). As a result of their strong grasp of these aspects of the Eucharist, some writers of today see, in its institution, the point at which the Church took its rise and, in the Eucharistic body, that which gives its name to the mystical Body itself.[1] For the same reason, theologians, both ancient and modern, are at one accord in seeing the unity of the mystical Body as the effect proper to the Sacrament of the Eucharist.[2]

There is one fact of exceptional importance that results from these considerations; it is that the constitution of the mystical Body at the deepest level of its being is the ground of sacramental action and of its causality. What exactly is sacramental action? It is a whole complex of things and gestures, of their very nature sensible and social, whereby our faith in Christ as Saviour is given expression and which, through a special efficaciousness attached by Christ to their symbolism, link us to the unique event of the redemption and salvation wrought by Christ in his death and resurrection. The sacraments are not, strictly speaking, new acts, but they are, in the spiritual mode of being, which is that of a celebration at once symbolical and real, the actual presence in his substance (in the Eucharist), or of his sanctifying power (in Baptism and the others), of Christ in his mystery of Redemption. When a man is baptised a Christian nothing is added to Christ. The act of baptising is not, in relation to the passion and resurrection, a strictly new action. What it does is to make these effectively profitable to the individual Christian, to include him expressly in the redemptive act done by Christ for him and to bring into his soul the fruit of reconciliation and of life resulting from the Passion, namely, communion with the Trinity, in whose name Baptism is conferred. Likewise, the

[1] Rawlinson, *Corpus Christi*, in *Mysterium Christi*, ed. Bell and Deissmann, London, 1930, pp. 225–244. St. Albert had already pointed out the connection between the name of mystical Body given to the Church and the eucharistic body of Christ.

[2] There are numerous relevant texts in practically every article of questions 73 onwards in the 3rd part of the *Summa*.

Eucharist does not begin anew Christ's sacrifice nor is it, as regards the cross, a new action, strictly speaking; but it makes Christ present again as victim offered so that his sacrifice is ever again repeated without ceasing to be unique and becomes, wherever Christians are gathered together, their own sacrifice and that of the Church, and the accomplishment by them of what was accomplished for them, once and for all, by Christ.

Thus, the real meaning and function of the sacraments is this, that by them Christians are placed in contact with Christ himself, their Redeemer, the one and the same Lord who, at a particular time, suffered and rose; that they receive the same life-giving sap that proceeds from the tree of the cross; in short, that the life by which they are to live is the very life of Christ. The sacraments are precisely the means by which is realized the oneness, nay the uniqueness, of the mediation of Christ. That justification by faith is both given and expressed by the rite of Baptism means that we are justified and become one of the faithful, in Christ, by the very fact of being sacramentally participators in his passion and resurrection. That the charity by which the soul enters fully into communication with the divine life is both given and expressed in the Eucharist, which is at once "Agape" and "Synaxis", means, and effects, that we are vivified and are made a single body in Christ. In every aspect, the sacrament signifies and effects that our divine life of faith and charity is mystically the life of Christ dead and resurrected, and that his mystery, in perfect truth, is lived mystically by the Church which is his Body.

Baptism and the Eucharist are, in both theology and the Christian life, the greatest of the sacraments. It is, of course, easy to find actions of Christ in his office of Messias and even certain passages of Scripture which bear on the other sacraments—for instance, the laying on of hands to give the fullness of the Holy Ghost or for the work of the ministry; the union of husband and wife as referring to the mystery of the union of Christ and the Church; the power of forgiving sins; the various anointings. All these sacraments relate to the constitution of the Church. They are signs, and signs which effect what they signify, of God's alliance with the Church. They all refer to Christ's passion which established this alliance, to the gift of his Spirit, which is the beginning of its realization in us and to the glory promised in the future, in which it will be finally perfected. This is what is expressed so succinctly and clearly by St. Thomas about the Eucharist: "Recolitur memoria passionis ejus, mens impletur gratia, et futurae gloriae nobis pignus datur".

We can see why it is that the early theologians, when they set about defining the Church, proposed, in addition to the rather more sociological one of "congregatio hominum fidelium"[1], this other, "Ecclesia, id est fides et fidei sacramenta".[2] What makes the Church is our faith and the sacraments in which it takes visible form. The Church is, of its essence, sacramental.

VI

Christ does not confine himself to sensible means of an inanimate nature for the formation of his mystical Body but uses, also, and for the same reason, living ones, persons who are themselves sacramental. The Church, then, is not only sacramental, but also apostolic and hierarchic (in the original sense of having sacred powers).

Christ was endowed by God with his power, in order to reconcile us and reunite us with him, in one body consisting of all the redeemed. The purpose on which he is henceforth engaged is to recapitulate in himself, for the glory of the Father, all the world he has gained over, the *populus acquisitionis* (1 Peter ii. 9), to take up into himself all that pertains to the first Adam, so that, made to the image of God and re-created to that of Christ, it may return to the model after which it was fashioned. Now, this work of recreation is performed by Christ through his Spirit in an invisible manner, but he does it also by visible means, by the sacraments, as we have seen, and by the ministry of men. So there

[1] Often occurring in St. Thomas—e.g. *In Symbol.*, a. 9; *Comp. theol.*, c. 147, etc.

[2] E.g. St. Thomas, *iv Sent.*, d. 17, q. 3, a. 1, sol. 5; *Sum. theol.*, iii, 64, 2 ad. 3, etc.

are, at work in the Church, activities performed, as it were, vicariously for that of Christ—the action of the Spirit, invisible and interior,[1] and that of the apostolic body, visible and exterior.[2] They are both closely connected, as we see at Pentecost and all through the Acts, for instance, in the calm announcement of the synod at Jerusalem, "It has seemed good to the Holy Ghost and to us . . ." (Acts xv. 28).

This is beyond dispute, as is also that Christ entrusted the task of building up *his* Church to *his* Spirit, who works interiorly, and, jointly with that Spirit, to the group of *his* apostles. Christ himself, strictly speaking, was the founder of the Church only in three respects—he accomplished in himself our redemption; he chose the apostles, instructing them and investing them with certain powers; he sent them into the world and, along with them, he sent his Spirit. Beyond that, he acts in the Church only through his apostles or jointly with them[3]. First there took place the imparting to Christ of the fullness of the Godhead and of Christ's fullness to the Church and, corresponding to this, there is another process, the visible mission, described, following St. John (xvii. 17–19; cf. xx. 21; Acts. ix. 4 and 1 Cor. iii. 23), by Clement (*Ad Cor.* xlii. 1–2) and Tertullian (*De Praescrip.*) on the words: the Father sends the Son, the Son sends the apostles. So we must always bear in mind that Christ's promise to be "with you all days even to the consummation of the world" (Mt. xxviii. 20) is fulfilled in two ways: he is in the Church by his Spirit, his Πνεῦμα, and he is present by his power. He is in his Church as animating it, by a spirit of holiness, to eternal life; he is there as acting in it through the agency of men invested with spiritual powers for the purpose of bringing his work to fulfilment.

1 "Christi vicarius"—Tertullian, *Praescr.*, c. 28.

2 Cf. preface for apostles—"operis tui vicarios".

3 Thus Christ, after appearing to St. Paul on the road to Damascus, told him: "Go into the city, and there it will be told you what you must do". Likewise, the voice said to Cornelius that he was to send for Peter and to listen to what he would say.

At the same time as he was proclaiming the coming of the kingdom, Christ chose out for himself a group of men whom he called apostles and which he formed for the service of this kingdom. He established them as leaders within the people he was to gather into the kingdom, judges of the twelve tribes of the new Israel (Luke. xxii. 19, etc.). In the Acts, their mission is seen to involve three kinds of activity—they bear witness, they are ministers of the sacred mysteries and they are heads of the various communities of the faithful.

(1) They are witnesses, by their preaching, of the salvation accomplished for us in Christ's passion and resurrection (Acts i. 17–22); they witness to the new alliance. Their mission it is to bring men to belief in Christ as Redeemer (John xvii. 20); they are sent to make disciplies of all nations and thereby bring them salvation (Mt. xxviii. 19–20; Mark xvi. 15–16). Just as the sacraments, as we have seen, are the means of bringing each individual Christian, in all ages and times, into relation with the single historical act of Christ's passion and resurrection, so the apostolic mission is the means of linking the salvation of each, on the basis of faith, to the unique historical fact of salvation, to the Christ of history, in whom alone there is salvation, and also to all he did for us "from the baptism of John" to his departure from our midst. Thus, far from being, over and above Christ, on an equal footing with him, means of salvation inclining us to place our confidence in human agency, the sacraments and the apostolic ministry make actual and show forth Christ's unique mediation. The Church, sacramental and apostolic in its very nature, is, in every aspect, the expression of the sole mediation of Christ who came in the flesh for our sakes.

(2) They are the ministers of the sacred mysteries, for by them the service of the kingdom is assured. Faith, indeed, is not the only condition of our entrance into the kingdom. According to St. John (iii. 5), there must be a new birth of water and the Spirit; and so Christ sent the apostles, not only to preach, but to baptise (Mt. xxviii. 19; Mark xvi. 16). They were to be "dispensers of

the mysteries of God" (1 Cor. iv. 1), to baptise, to celebrate the Eucharist, to lay on hands. Moreover, they soon handed on to others the charge of performing many of these functions, of baptising, of anointing the sick (James v. 14), of the Eucharist; but they kept to themselves the imposition of hands for communicating the fullness of the Holy Spirit (Acts viii. 14 sq.; xviii. 24; xix, etc.). In this regard, we possess, in early documents, a whole assemblage of facts whose meaning is perfectly clear and which, very early on, with St. Irenaeus, are expressed by the idea of "apostolic succession". This idea, according to a modern critic, is presupposed all through the Acts. It was not long after the time of the apostles before Clement of Rome, in the lifetime of the last of them, wrote: "Acting on the instructions of Our Lord Jesus Christ, and fully convinced by the fact of his resurrection, the apostles, strengthened by the word of God, went forth, in the power of the Holy Ghost, to proclaim the good news, the coming of the kingdom of God. After having preached in towns and in the country places, they made trial in the Holy Ghost of their first converts, the fruit of their work, and instituted them as bishops and deacons of the future believers. . . . Our apostles also knew, by Our Lord Jesus Christ, that disputes would arise about the episcopal dignity. For that reason, in their clear insight into the future, they instituted those we have already spoken of, and then laid down the rule that, after their death, other proven men should succeed to their ministry. Those who were thus put in charge by the apostles, or later by other persons of eminence, with the approval of the whole Church. . . ." (*Ad Cor.* xlii. 3–4; xliv. 1 sq.).

(3) They are the heads of the various communities of the faithful, being so constituted by their teaching-function (cf. Heb. xiii. 7), and these communities themselves usually considered, as the example of Corinth shows, that their supreme ruler was the apostle who first brought them to the knowledge of the Lord. But, though an apostle like St. Paul held authority over all the Churches, he was obviously unable to govern in person even

those founded by himself (cf. Acts xiv. 23; xx. 28; Titus i. 5, etc.). This is shown in countless texts, and the pastoral epistles, whatever view we take as to their mode of composition, present, towards the end of the apostolic period, a Church well on the way to a hierarchical organization deriving from the authority of the apostles.

The classical division of the acts of this authority, from the standpoint of the government of the communities, is into legislative, judicial and punitive ones. The words themselves are, of course, foreign to the terminology of the time, but not far removed from it, and, in any case, what they indicated subsequently is already to be found everywhere in the New Testament writings. We will just point out a few representative passages—of the legislative power: "It is seemed good to the Holy Ghost and to us . . ." (Acts xv. 28), "the precept holds, which is the Lord's precept and not mine. . . . I give my own instructions, not the Lord's . . ." (1 Cor. vii. 10, 12); of the judicial power: ". . . . with all the power of Our Lord Jesus Christ . . . ." (1 Cor. v. 4), and the power of defining clearly the bounds of a jurisdiction which extends only to the baptised (1 Cor. v. 12); finally of the power of punishing, even of excommunicating (1 Cor. v., etc.), with the consciousness of thereby doing the work and executing the will of the Lord (Mt. xviii. 17).

Thus the constitution of the Church as the mystical Body which we have seen to be essentially sacramental is clearly, at the same time, essentially apostolic. For we must fully realize that the aim of the triple function, doctrinal, ministerial and pastoral, of the apostles is not the order of any kind of society, but the actual realization of the mystical Body. Their preaching is itself the act which, by arousing faith in their hearers and providing it with its object, opens up the way to salvation (cf. Acts xx. 32; Rom. x. 14 sq.; 1 Cor. iii. 5; 2 Thess. ii. 13–14—all most forcible). This salvation is given by their ministry, which is one of reconciliation (2 Cor. v. 18 sq.; cf. iii. 9), a service of the spirit (2 Cor. iii. 6; Gal. iii. 5), a building up of the body of Christ (Eph. iv. 12), which grows up in charity, built up in the framework of the hierarchical functions (Eph. ii. 19–22; iv. 6; Col. ii. 19, etc.); salvation, entrance into the kingdom, the life of the heavenly city, are an essentially apostolic thing that is bound up with the ministry of the apostles, and subsequently of their successors. So it is that St. John, in the Apocalypse, represents the heavenly Jerusalem as having twelve gates, and its walls as founded on twelve stones on which are written twelve names, those of the twelve apostles of the Lamb (Apoc. xxi. 12, 14; cf. 3 Kings xviii. 30 sq.). Our Lord's words, reported by the same apostle, "I am the door of the sheep . . ." (John x. 7 sq.), do not contradict this, for, if Christ is the shepherd of souls, it is also true that the apostolic body received from him the same function (1 Peter v. 2 sq.); so that Christ's will, proclaimed by him, that there should be one flock and one shepherd (John x. 16) is to have its spiritual fulfilment in Christ, and its apostolic fulfilment in the visible Church.

The apostolic body, in fact, evidently discharged, in the Church, the function of an organ and of a criterion of its unity, a unity which was always conceived as visible and social. Recent studies have brought out most clearly the important part in the unity of the Church played, at the outset of its expansion, by the community at Jerusalem, where the apostolic college dwelt for a fairly long time. The community of the saints in Jerusalem was the basis and criterion of unity; to be conformed with it and remain united to it was to abide in unity; to be disowned by it, by the apostolic college and, especially, by those who were "pillars", was to have "run in vain" (Gal. ii. 2). The Church had been built on the apostles; and, as it spread, if it wished to remain one while becoming Catholic, it had to remain strictly apostolic, the apostles thus becoming, as it were, a criterion for the preservation of unity in the course of expansion. We are thinking here not only of geographical expansion, but of every kind of growth—institution, doctrinal—of a body that is alive.

Yet, though the group of apostles is the criterion of unity, there is one who, within their number, had received a function of initiation, representation, the power to preside and make decisions. All the New Testament passages, even that in which St. Paul speaks of the appearances of Christ (1 Cor. xv. 5 sq.), proclaim that an undoubted primacy was given to Peter, a primacy not of love, which belonged to John, nor merely of honour, but a primacy in the actual exercise of the apostolate entrusted to the twelve and in the role of criterion held by the apostles to keep intact the unity of the body. The actual texts bearing on this primacy (Mt. xvi. 15–20; Luke xxii. 31–32; John xxi. 15–17) are to be understood in this light, and so also the primacy of the apostolic See.

For the Catholic Church holds that just as the apostolicity of the Church is always in being and as the function of the apostolic body continues in the episcopate, so the function of Peter as criterion within the apostolic body for the preservation of the Church in unity continues in the See of Peter, that of Rome. It is not our purpose here to present, still less to discuss, the texts and the events on which this claim rests. We will quote only the following, from H. B. Swete's *The Holy Catholic Church*, (1915, p. 20, n. 2): "From the second century onwards a catena of testimony makes and acknowledges the claims of the Roman Church to be, through its connexion with S. Peter and S. Paul, in a special sense, the depositary and guardian of an apostolic tradition, a type and model for other churches". Still earlier than the second century, the epistle known as that of Clement to the Church of Corinth, and certain converging facts, are, if not proofs, at least indications showing that the Catholic position is something more than a challenge offered to history.

VII

Besides being sacramental and apostolic in its nature, the Church is also social; it has the form and satisfies the requirements of a society.

The Church is the new Israel; and, like the Israel of old, it is a people of God with its own corporate life, its laws and its hierarchy. The early Christians were fully aware of their status as the new Israel formed by God, not in the framework of the twelve tribes, a racial one, but in that of the four corners of the world, under the judicial authority of the twelve apostles. The pagans, in fact, derided them on that account, calling them a *tertium genus*.[1] If we read quite simply the New Testament texts and the earliest Christian writings of the time before the peace of Constantine we are struck by the plainness and absence of distinctions with which the mystical Body of Christ and the Church in its social being are identified as a single reality. The mystical Body is not some spiritual entity unrelated to the world of human realities and activities but it is the visible Church itself; it can no more be dissociated from this than, say, France considered in its spiritual reality can be dissociated in fact from the institutions and realities of the visible France, with its laws, constitution, government, and so forth. Fortunately, in these days we are well free of the tendency of reading into the ancient documents the modern liberal religion "of the spirit", or interpreting them from the Lutheran standpoint of a dissociation between the visible and the invisible Church. Kattenbusch, in particular, shows, in *Der Quellort*, that, if the Church was, for the first generations of Christians, a coming down of heaven upon earth, if it was a mutual *Ineinandersein* of Christ and Christians, it was, at the same time and inseparably, *Societas fidei et Spiritus Sancti in cordibus*, and *Societas externarum rerum et rituum*.

A few verses of the Acts (ii. 42–47) provide unimpeachable evidence of the life of the Church in the very first years, and acquaint us with four of the characteristic actions of the new people of God.

"They occupied themselves continually", we are told, "with the apostles' teaching". They were not just a number of enlightened individuals forming themselves into a community, but

[1] Awareness of being the new Israel—Rom. ix. 6; 1 Cor. x. 18; Gal. vi. 16; cf. James i. 1. Cf. Ramsey, *op. cit.*, chs. 1 and 2; C. A. Lacey, *Unity and Schism*, 1, les., and pp. 137 sq. ("The Church is a civic unit", p. 24).

something more like a "Church taught" informed by a "teaching Church". They were occupied "in fellowship", that is to say, apparently, in a life in common which, in those early times, generally went as far as a community in material possessions, a mode of life in which the Christian spirit was carried to its furthest extreme—at any rate, it was a social way of life, under the direction and control of the apostles, and one which, before long, required a special hierarchical institution, that of deacons. "They occupied themselves continually . . . in the breaking of bread", which, if it does not signify exclusively the Eucharist, at least implies it (cf. Acts xx. 7). Finally, "they occupied themselves continually . . . with the fixed times of prayer", that is, as verse 46 points out, in the temple. These activities in common, at which the apostles presided, resulted in there being "one heart and soul in all the company of believers" (Acts iv. 32).

Obviously, various factors, human, geographical, cultural, historical, soon brought about in this ecclesial life developments, modifications, adaptations. When the Church went out from Jerusalem and penetrated the Greek world; when it reached an age when men no longer had known Christ or the apostles, or even the immediate disciples of these; when it extended over the whole *Imperium Romanum*, and then, later on, beyond it; when it left the catacombs for the Constantinian basilicas; when it subdued kings, established Christendom, and enjoyed a virtual monopoly of culture . . . it obviously had to take on external forms other than those of the community just come into being after Pentecost, presided over by the apostles, whose membership still included the Mother and brethren of the Lord.

None the less, there still remain the same elements of the ecclesial communion, making of all Christians a single heart and soul; a witnessing to the Incarnation and Redemption, given by a hierarchical body which continues the witness of the apostles, and received by the faithful in that unanimity of sentiment and expression demanded of them by St. Paul (1 Cor. i. 10; 1 Tim. iv., etc.); a community of life, mutual help and edification, a realization, at every level, of the *communio sanctorum*, social and religious life being so bound up together that St. Paul[1] and the earliest writers[2] are ever recurring to the idea of a Christian life led as a community, a life of members in one body, each contributing his share to the progress of the whole[3], which is Christ; participation in the sacraments and, above all, after Baptism, which gives membership in the Church, of the Eucharist, round which the whole liturgy is organized as its natural flowering.

The Christian life is a life in Christ which is nourished, maintained and expressed in a spiritual life of a social and strictly ecclesiastical nature; union with Christ, which is the interior life of the individual soul, is lived and acquired socially, in the Church. Thus, within the Church, the spiritual realities of the *vita in Christo* possess a social and strictly ecclesiastical form wherein they are expressed, embodied and nourished—there, union with the mystery of Christ's redemption is Baptism, the Eucharist and the other sacraments; faith is expressed and nourished in dogma, piety likewise in the liturgy; love, which results in mutual help and service, is strengthened and sustained by submission to law; the three chief elements of the ecclesiastical communion are both served and directed by a hierarchy invested with the threefold power of the magisterium, the priesthood and pastoral governance. All this goes to constitute a single Church both spiritually and externally one, the centre of the personal union of souls with God, and the social embodiment of life in Christ—a body in which, in the words of St. Irenaeus, "disposita est communicatio Christi" (*Haer.* iii. 24, 1).

[1] E.g. Mutual help—Rom. xv, 25 sq.; xvi, 2; Gal. v. 13; 1 Thess. iii, 12; 2 Thess. i. 3; cf. 1 Peter ii. 13–14. Mutual edification—Rom. xii. 9 sq.; xiv. 19; xv. 2; 1 Cor. viii. 9 sq. and 20–22; x. 23 and 32–33; Col. iii. 3, etc.

[2] E.g. Clement, Ad. Cor. xxxvii. 5, and xxxviii. 1; Ignatius, *Magn.* xiii. 2; Polycarp, *Phil.* x. 2.

[3] See 1 Cor. xii, 4–30, etc. The practice of public penance in Christian antiquity shows that the sins of individuals were looked on as impairing the spiritual good of the whole society. The interior state of the soul was not dissociated from the common good of the Church.

VIII

Being of its very nature a society, the Church must be constituted accordingly, that is to say, there must be in it a certain arrangement of powers and functions corresponding to the kind of co-operation and unity demanded by its own special nature and the well-being of its members.

In one sense, then, the Church is a society like any other, since it has a social structure and we see in it, as in all societies, public authority, law, sanctions, public acts and subjects governed. Yet, at the same time, it is not as human societies are; its nature and its "common good" are of quite a different kind. It is, in fact, the "mystical Body", and its common good consists in the divine life communicated to mankind in Christ through faith and the sacraments of faith.

(1) First of all, in the Church the "powers" are not quite what they are in a political society. The latter does not constitute its members in existence, but takes them over from the family and its whole function in their regard is to co-ordinate activities they are already capable of performing, in view of a "common good". Moreover, a political society requires of its subjects only a practical conformity; it may not teach, still less impose, truths of the speculative order, any view of things taken in themselves. Consequently, it possesses, over its subjects, only a power of governing (i.e. legislative, executive and coercive), in other words, of direction towards an end. The Church, however, before exercising governmental authority over its subjects, has to constitute them such by giving them a mode of being they had not previously possessed, a being, that is, according to the new creation and that life in Christ of which Baptism is the beginning. Further, the Church is a society which lives essentially by the truth; not that it is a learned society or a kind of academy, but because it is a life with God on the basis of what God has himself communicated to us of his mystery in a supernatural revelation. Consequently, it has, besides a pastoral power of governing, a sacerdotal power of sanctifying and a prophetical power of

teaching—a jurisdiction, order and magisterium derived from the fullness of power of him who, as the way, the truth and the life, king, priest and prophet, wills to bring all men to their perfection in God.

(2) This brings us to a second difference between the society which is the Church and political society. The latter derives its powers immediately from the requirements and claims of the common good which they secure. The powers of the Church, however, come to it directly from Christ, and the Church exercises them solely in the name of Christ, who remains always its actual head. The apostles and Peter and, after them, the episcopal body united to the apostolic See, are not Christ's successors; they are only his vicars; that is to say, they receive from him a power of attorney during his absence, while, all the time, he remains the master. In any case, what do we mean by "during his absence"? Christ is not absent from the Church, indeed, spiritually, but he is absent corporally and visibly, and it is only in this aspect that the hierarchy continues and represents him vicariously, rather as the eucharistic species serve his bodily presence only from the point of view of visibility and localization.

Moreover, there are several distinctions to be drawn in this connection, for the vicarial relation to Christ is not quite the same for each of the three powers we have named. Whenever St. Paul or the hierarchy legislate, command or punish in accordance with their power of spiritual jurisdiction, they do so in the name of the Lord and make use of the powers received from him; but they decide themselves, freely, what they do, and use a power really given to them, one which resides in them and of which they dispose, within certain limits, absolutely. But when St. Paul or the hierarchy celebrate the mysteries or announce the word of God, they act in a much closer dependence on Christ; they no longer act by a power that truly resides in them, and they are by no means free, at least as regards the essential, to do one thing or another as they please. Here, as the scholastics say, they are instrumental causes, acting under complete dependence on him who uses them. That, indeed, is why they are able to announce a truth which is truly a word of God, and to perform sacramental acts (consecration, absolution, etc.) which involve the divine agency and, in fact, can only come from this. These distinctions are simple enough, but they are of great importance for the exact understanding of the powers and acts of the hierarchy—of such things as infallibility, indulgences, matrimonial legislation, conditions for reception of the sacraments and so on.

(3) The Church's powers come to it from Christ as those of Christ come to him from God. Consequently, through the whole range of its activities, there is always observed what might be called the law of hierarchical procession. Everything therein comes from above, from the bosom of the Father, through Christ and the apostles. The whole external order, therefore, of its constitution and life is an application, as well as a sensible representation, of the law according to which all it has comes from above. That is the inner meaning of the whole ordering of the consecrations, the sacraments, the liturgy, teaching and even of jurisdiction, where it is always a matter of communication from above to beneath, hierarchically. Those who speak disparagingly of human intermediaries and sacerdotalism may, indeed, show their keen sense of certain evangelical values, such as liberty and the interior spirit; but often enough they show a failure to grasp how, in the Church, all comes from above and how the Church itself is the great and universal sacrament of the sole mediation of Christ.

(4) Finally, the Church differs most profoundly from political society in that it is not a "body" only in the sense of a *corpus politicum*, but also, in mysterious fashion, in that of a *corpus organicum* or *biologicum*. It is not only a unity of order or of cooperation, like a natural society, but a unity of life, rather like that of a living body. This is of the greatest importance and a number of consequences follow. One of these is that the Church, strictly speaking, does not possess its law and constitution outside itself, but within, as a living being does. We are not to think of

the Church's essential law or constitution as we think of those of the political societies of our world. As regards these, it is a matter of constructing the state after the pattern of certain ideas, for example, according to the ideas of Marx; the constitution of the state exists, first of all, as an idea or document and one sets out to conform the reality to this. It is quite otherwise with a living thing; it bears its own law within itself and does not realize it according to a written scheme or an ideal constitution. It is self-realizing, it develops what it received in germ from its begetter, and can no more escape from its law, interior as it is, than one can leap outside one's own shadow.

It is roughly the same with the Church, and the circumstance is of great importance. Our Lord did not found it after the fashion of Solon, Lycurgus or Lenin, giving it a charter or a constitution. He founded it by giving its very being and life, promising it his Spirit to animate and assist it. He announced that, in virtue of living within it, we would have in it truth and life, because he would live in it himself, who is the way and the truth, by his Spirit.

Consequently, we Catholics presuppose the Church's fidelity to itself, to its essential law which lives in it by the power of Christ. We are quite aware that the Church has taken on, in the course of time, a great variety of external forms in which everything has not always been pure and irreproachable and which bear only a remote resemblance to the primitive or early forms. We believe, for example, in the permanent primacy of the apostolic See, and yet we know that between the form taken in the time of St. Clement and its form in that of St. Leo, St. Gegory VII, or St. Pius V, there are vast differences of modality. We believe in the existence of the sacrament of Penance in the earliest days of the Church, but we know that there are very great differences between the public penance of the time of the martyrs and our present practice of Confession. Similarly, we recognize a real continuity and homogeneity between the highly developed trinitarian, sacramental or ecclesiological doctrines and the very simple, though rich and pregnant, statements of the Gospels or the apostolic tradition. We are far from refusing to examine these questions critically or to explore their history; but we hold that these matters are delivered to us otherwise than in documents, that they are given in their living reality and that, in consequence, our faith goes beyond what a historian is able to read for himself in the documents and reaches to a reality given in the Church assisted, for the purpose of declaring it to us, by the Spirit of the Lord.

IX

Though we possess in advance the certainty that the Church as such will ever be the same by reason of its fidelity, as a living entity, to the interior law of its being, we clearly have no similar guarantee for the individual activity of men within the Church. The Spirit of Christ vivifies the Spouse of Christ and it is impossible for her, as such and taken in her totality, to fall short of complete fidelity. But individuals within her, and even her visible head acting as an individual[1], are fallible in various ways, and have often erred. We need to acknowledge the faults and infidelities of churchmen, especially the responsibility of the clergy and, more particularly, that of the Roman Curia for the terrible catastrophe of the Reformation.[2]

We believe, too, that the Church's doctrine is pure and unalloyed and that it contains the pure and simple truth in opposition to the various errors of each age. But we know—and this is at the basis of doctrinal progress—that the dogmas successively defined express the truth only partially. Dogmatic definitions are much more defensive reactions than positive and irenic teachings. The Church teaches in a variety of ways, by

1 The early theologians were unanimous in holding, not only that the Pope is capable of sin, that goes without saying, but that, as a private person, he may be heretical. In any case, there are the well-known cases of Honorius I and John XXII.

2 No one expressed this responsibility more strongly than the reformist Catholic bishops of the sixteenth century, such as Adrian VI and Cardinal Pole. See Pastor's *History of the Popes*, vol. 4.

catechisms, preaching, the liturgy, ecclesiastical life and practice; and it is in this ordinary teaching that her thought is chiefly to be looked for. Solemn definitions were nearly always made in opposition to particular errors and put forward only one aspect, sometimes not even the deepest or the most significant, of the truth. This is the case, especially, of the ecclesiological definitions of the Vatican Council, where for reasons quite foreign to the intentions of the Fathers of the Council, the Pope's primacy of jurisdiction and infallibility were the only matters defined. It must, however, be admitted that the fears aroused of a diminution and a virtual annihilation of the episcopacy have not been realized, and that official explanations of the dogmas have been given which, without minimising them, show the limited nature of their range.[1]

But in general it must be acknowledged that the theological treatise *De Ecclesia* was drawn up in very adverse circumstances. It was the outcome of the successive needs of defence against Gallicanism (fourteenth to fifteenth, and seventeenth centuries) and Protestantism; and so became an apologetical weapon, and the points attacked are practically the only ones developed and even then often one-sidedly. Hence arose the preponderance of questions, important in themselves, of course, concerning the Church's independence of the civil power, its hierarchical constitution, the primacy and *magisterium* of the Roman See, etc.

The study of the mystery of the inmost nature of the Church and of the deepest aspects of ecclesiological reality are not a recent innovation. Already in the nineteenth century Moehler, Pilgram and Franzelin had written profoundly on the divine and human mystery of the Church. But the present time is one of the greatest promise, a promise indeed already realized in part, for ecclesiological studies. At a deeper level, too, than that of theology, in the actual life of the Church there is going on, in these days, a transformation whose development and ultimate consequences

[1] Cf. Abbot Butler, *The Vatican Council*, London, 1930.

it is impossible to foresee. Starting from the order given by Pius X at the very height of the modernist crisis, *Instaurare omnia in Christo*, a succession of movements has appeared like a great stirring in the depths of the sea and continues to develop—a liturgical movement, a mystical movement, a missionary movement, a communal apostolic movement and a theological movement. The liturgical movement was well in being before the first war; the mystical renewal took definite form in the years immediately following; the missionary movement, prepared by Benedict XV, was especially fostered by Pius XI, who also gave the communal apostolic movement the form of Catholic Action, that is to say of an apostolate of the laity in their own special surroundings—it has already yielded, particularly in the Young Christian Workers, a splendid harvest of fields won for Christ and of a pure, deep and generous interior life. Finally, the theological movement though of its nature, hardly at all institutional, is yet strongly pronounced and shows a clear resolve to go beyond the unilateral and often ossified post-Tridentine theology, and to go back to the great medieval syntheses and the great sources of the patristic age and the scriptural revelation.

X

By way of rounding off this study and summing up what has been said, we will look at the actual reality of the Church and its unity as it appears to the observer.

The Church shows itself, in the first place, as a corporate mode of life which adapts itself, in some degree, to the progress of human society but which has its own rhythm, its particular existence, its laws, usages, rites, organization, works and its own hierarchy. Those who share in this life live in a parochial community where all its acts take place—birth followed by baptism, childhood with the first catechetical instruction and first Communion, Sunday Mass, various religious functions, festival solemnities, special sermons, marriages, initiation of each new generation to prayer and the sacraments, funerals, anointing of the sick and viaticum.

In the parish, there is a man who officiates at public worship, administers the sacraments, teaches doctrine, gives advice, sees to the observance of Christian duties and the "laws of the Church". For whoever claims to be a believer is bound to certain practices and to the acceptance of a fairly considerable body of doctrines.

Above the parish, a priest of higher rank, invested with more extensive powers and in command of the others, is the upholder and expression of a larger unity, that of the diocese. But the religious community does not stop there, nor even at the whole aggregate of believers in the country. All Catholics throughout the world, regardless of differences in race, language, culture and place, acknowledge themselves to be a single people, living the same life, sustained by the same hopes. One man, again, is the upholder of this unity and, at the same time, its symbol, one whom all call "the Holy Father". If such a multitude, differing in so many ways, lives truly in unity, it is because the Church has in him its visible head, its criterion of unity; he is obeyed as the visible Vicar of Jesus Christ.

All this, organization, laws and customs, rites and sacraments, works and joint efforts of every kind, has but one end, to further, beyond all human possibility or likelihood, a life of faith and love hidden in God with Christ. All this ceremonial observance, the whole build-up, exists for no other cause than to arouse in the world faith and love for Christ and God. The claims made by the Church, its fierce insistence on its right to the education of children, its intransigence on doctrine and extreme reserve in regard to innovations, all has one aim, to unite souls to God by making them, through faith, the sacraments of faith, and love, living members of the mystical Body of Christ. This Church, in fact, organized for action and powerfully constituted as a society, is, seen from within, a community living mystically with the dead, risen and glorified Christ. The juridical implications of the ecclesiastical community have certainly developed in the Church but it is, none the less, no different in substance from the community in the cenacle which, intent on the preaching of the apostles, the common life, the breaking of bread and prayer, had but one heart and soul in Christ. Now as then there exists the assemblage of those called by God to be the beneficiaries of his heritage, with the saints, in light. All its exterior life, all its social ordering, are but an expression and an instrument of an interior life which is the life of Christ. The whole external and visible activity of the Church goes to realize what is, indeed, its inner essence, the life of all mankind in Christ.

III

The Idea of the Church in St. Thomas Aquinas

IT WAS customary to say, at least until recent years, that there was no treatise on the Church in St. Thomas and to place the origin of this treatise in the fifteenth century with the *Summa de Ecclesia* of the Dominican Cardinal, John Turrecremata. Historians have recently claimed for the treatise a more ancient origin, and with justice. Arquillière, in his edition of the *De Regimine Christiano* of James of Viterbo, describes it as "the most ancient treatise on the Church". He is indisputably right in reclaiming priority for this work—older than the *Summa* of Turrecremata by nearly one hundred and fifty years; but he adds in his turn: "This phrase [elaboration of the treatise *De Ecclesia*] means that, for the first time, theological speculation strives, not to define the Church (for that had been done in the first centuries), but to discuss with a greater span its distinctive marks, its organization in the form of a kingdom, and the authority which rules it". Arquillière here makes an important distinction: if the *De Regimine Christiano* of James of Viterbo appears as the first treatise on the Church, then before it there was no treatise of its *kind*. This assertion obviously rests on a criterion; it involves a certain notion of what constitutes a treatise on the Church and further of what the Church herself is. The assertion is one that is typical of a certain concept of the Church which developed in the age of James of Viterbo, in the disputes with Philippe le Bel; in the age of Turrecremata, in the midst of the arguments about the Council and the Pope raised by the Great Schism; and then in the age of the Reformation, as a reaction against the denial of every kind of institutional and visible Church by Protestantism. And yet it is just this idea of the Church which is now called into question and made subject to revision by that present movement of thought and life which represents, as a whole, a return to something earlier than the polemic anti-gallican and anti-Protestant positions, a return to the infinitely wider and deeper viewpoints of the great theological traditions of the Fathers and the great scholastics, and in particular to that of St. Thomas.

It is true that on the Church St. Thomas wrote no separate treatise, characterized by a study of the distinctive marks of the Church, of its organization in the form of kingdom, or of the authority which rules it. But it seems quite clear that St. Thomas has in his works answers to these questions, answers which are precise enough even though scattered. It has even been said, and perhaps truly, that he was the first to introduce into theology a doctrine of papal infallibility; above all, it appears quite certain that his works contain scattered but most explicit principles of a theology of the Church *having a different drift* from that which developed subsequently, and it is even conceivable—the writer, indeed, is strongly inclined to the opinion—that St. Thomas acted deliberately when he wrote no separate treatise on the Church but conceived one on the lines which shall be set forth in the following.

But just one introductory note: all I say here about St. Thomas is equally true of St. Bonaventure, Alexander of Hales, Albert the Great and the other scholastics of that epoch. Excluding certain delicate distinctions which do not affect the general structural outlines, all these scholastics offer the same ecclesiology as St. Thomas. In short, before the "first treatises on the Church", no other method was known.

Examined closely, the ecclesiological tests of St. Thomas are numerous, but to begin with it is enough to choose them haphazardly. Still, there is one which I prefer to take as a starting point, not only because it is one of the most thorough, but also because it occurs in a work where St. Thomas, speaking expressly about the Church herself, was more free to develop his thought as he wished without being bound or determined by considerations of systematic construction: the subject being the explanation of the words: *Sanctam Ecclesiam Catholicam*, in the *Expositio in Symbolum* (where St. Thomas follows the text, not of the Creed of Nicea-Constantinople, the *Symbolum Patrum*, but of the so-called Apostles' Creed). I give this text almost in its entirety:

> As in a man there is one soul and one body, yet a diversity of members, so the Catholic Church is one body and has different members. The soul which quickens this body is the Holy Ghost; and that is why, after faith in the Holy Ghost, we are required to have faith in the Catholic Church, as the Creed itself makes clear. He who says Church says Congregation; and he who says Holy Church says Congregation of the Faithful; and he who says Christian Man says Member of that Church. . . . The Church is one, and this unity of the Church is grounded in three elements. It is grounded first in the oneness of faith; for all Christians belonging to the body of the Church believe in the same reality, as Scripture says: *That ye all speak the same thing, and that there be no divisions among you* (1 Cor. i. 10); *One Lord, one faith, one baptism* (Eph. iv. 5). Further, this unity comes from the oneness of hope, for all are rooted in the same hope of attaining to eternal life, as St. Paul says again: *There is one body, and one Spirit, even as ye are called in one hope of your calling* (Eph. iv. 4). Thirdly, there is the oneness in love, love of one another, according to what St. John says: *The glory which thou gavest me I have given them; that they may be one, even as we are one* (John xvii. 22). This love reveals itself, if it be true, when the members have care and solicitude one for another and when they feel for one

another. . . . The Church of Christ is holy . . . with a holiness which is grounded in three things . . . in this, that the faithful have been washed in the Blood of Christ . . . in that spiritual anointing which they have received and whereby they have been sanctified . . . which anointing is the grace of the Holy Ghost . . . and thirdly in the fact that the Trinity dwells in her . . . in short, that there we call upon the name of the Lord. . . . Furthermore, the Church is Catholic, that is, Universal. First in virtue of her spatial or geographic Catholicity, which springs from her diffusion through the whole world . . . then from the Catholicity which she has by inclusion of all kinds and conditions of men of which none is left without . . . lastly, she is universal in time . . . enduring from Abel till the end of the world, after which she shall continue to endure in heaven. . . . Fourthly, the Church is indestructible . . . having Christ for her chief foundation and the Apostles and their doctrine for the second . . . and that is why she is called apostolic. . . .

In this text, where St. Thomas and his thought are not conditioned by any particular biblical passage, by any question of systematic articulation, but have free play, we find him defining the Church as a living body compacted out of a plurality of members, all quickened and governed by a single living principle. This living principle or soul is the Holy Ghost. In a more immediate manner, the various members of this living body which is the Church are a unity in virtue not only of the indwelling of God in them, the indwelling of the Trinity, and the possession of the Holy Ghost, not only in virtue of the presence of this divine soul which dwells in them—one of the titles of the Church's claim of holiness—but also in virtue of the fact that God, always through the possession of the Holy Ghost, places *in them* certain tendencies, which flow from Him into them as gifts or graces and which in them are the virtues of faith, hope, and love. The Church is one living body, not only because a single soul dwells therein and makes a temple of it, but also because a single soul, namely, the theological virtues, which are divine life immanent in men, quickens its members inwardly.

To clarify these general ideas which dominate St. Thomas' notion of the Church, the following points must be noted:

(1) Admittedly, the corporative idea throws much light on many aspects of his view of the Church. Yet if the Church is a "body" it is not only in the sociological sense of the word defined by St. Thomas as "a multiplicity organized into unity by the concourse of different activities and functions"; rather it is conceived in a manner which must remain profoundly mysterious, in the biological sense of the word. When St. Thomas inquires into the nature of the law which operates in the economy of the New Covenant, he finds that it is before all else the grace of the Holy Spirit: that is to say, not a text or a sociological structure, but an inward reality, a supernatural living thing.

(2) Nevertheless, this life does not dissolve us in God; it is, indeed, a wonderful thing that, while living by the life of God, we are able to be and to remain personalities; it is genuinely *we ourselves* who live by this life. The unity which grafts us into God is a social unity of personalities, after the pattern of the Triune Society of the Absolute. The mode of our living by the divine life is the mode of spirits, of persons. Moreover, life is determined like all movement, by its objects; for men to live the life of means having the "ends" and objects of the life of God: this is achieved by the theological virtues, by faith which begins to see as God sees, love which loves as God loves, and by all the moral virtues. To define the Church as a body having community of life with God is to conceive of it as humanity vitalized Godwards by the theological virtues, which have God for their object, and organized in the likeness of God by the moral virtues. The ecclesiology of St. Thomas is profoundly *ex unitate fidei quia idem credunt, ex unitate spei quia omnes sperant vitam aeternam, ex unitate caritatis quia omnes connectuntur in amore Dei;* she is one because, by faith, hope, and love, all have the same vital object and goal, and because this is itself the very object *of the life of God.* Hence

it is also true to say that the entire *Secunda Pars* of the *Summa Theologica* is ecclesiology.

(3) The plane or sphere of means and ends must correspond. Only God can lift us up to the life of God; only a "dynamic" principle genuinely divine can direct and move us towards the objects of the divine life. So also, St. Thomas tells us that the Holy Ghost is the quickening soul of the body of men living by the life of God. This is a characteristic and classic idea in the patristic and scholastic tradition, but one which St. Thomas has vividly portrayed and which, far from being a mere pious metaphor, a literary flourish or nebulous exaggeration, manifests and represents a powerful technical factor in his theological thought. I shall recall three examples and no more, but these are tremendously significant ones. In chapters 20, 21 and 22 of the Fourth Book of the *Contra Gentiles,* St. Thomas explains how and why the whole supernatural life of man, the whole *motus creaturae in Deum,* is to be attributed to the Holy Ghost. This idea is most clearly developed in the question of merit which, to be most exact, is the efficacious power in the moral action of the spiritual life of man, of attaining *God,* his final end. Realizing that only what comes effectively from God can return efficaciously to Him, attaining to Him, and appealing to the words of Christ in the Gospel of St. John, *Fiet in eo fons aquae salientis in vitam aeternam* (John iv. 14), St. Thomas sees that merit depends on two conditions: first, the meritorious act is free, really emanating from us (remember that we are discussing a society of *persons*); secondly, it receives its meritorious efficacy from God, *ex hoc quod procedit ex gratia Spiritus Sancti, secundum virtutem Spiritus Sancti moventis nos in vitam aeternam.* Lastly, if we look at the Sacraments, which confer this grace efficaciously, we see that St. Thomas relates their efficacy to the power of the Holy Ghost working within them: "The water of Baptism receives its efficacy from . . . the Holy Ghost, as from its first cause, says St. Paul. This can be understood . . . in a second sense of the sacramental drink, which the Holy Ghost consecrates". And the same applies to all the functions

and ministries of the Church, whose efficacy St. Thomas traces to the Holy Ghost, who is indeed the soul of the Church, the dynamic power of this life of humanity moving Godwards. Herein St. Thomas sees the first and deepest notion that can be had of the Church.

To sum up this first glance at the mystery of the Church contemplated in not a few texts of St. Thomas, but mainly in his commentary on the Creed, we may say that it is anthropological or moral, and pneumatological or theocentric. The substance of the Church is made of the new life which men receive by the three virtues of faith, hope and love and which is a life driven Godwards, which has God for its end, and the objects of divine life as its determining principles. For St. Thomas, the Church is the whole economy of the return towards God, *motus rationalis creaturae in Deum*, in short, the *Secunda Pars* of his *Summa Theologica*. Of this *motus* and return the Holy Ghost is the power and agent; He is the principle of this divine life which is determined by the "dynamism" towards the objects of the life of God; He is the soul of the Church.

To this elemental notion corresponds the definition of the Church, classic in ancient theology, as *Congregatio Fidelium*: the assembly of those who have received the gift of faith and, through it, have been made sharers of the divine life.

* * *

If the Church is the economy of the return of personal beings to God, *reditus creaturae rationalis in Deum*, this return can only be accomplished actually *in Christo, qui, secundum quod homo, via est nobis tendendi in Deum*. I have already said that the ecclesiology of St. Thomas, like the ethic to which it is wedded, is *above all things* theocentric, and the same may be said of the ecclesiology of St. Paul. It is inevitable that to try to think of the mystery of the Church in the light of the principles of St. Thomas means focusing the attention first on the theocentric aspect and only after that on the Christocentric. Further, in the two systematic expositions of theology which he has left us—both of them unfinished—St. Thomas brings out the theocentric aspect before the Christocentric one.

And yet, the second aspect is in nowise minimized or blurred by the first, and after having found in the commentary on the Creed a first notion both anthropological or moral and pneumatological or theocentric, we read on and find in St. Thomas a strong christological idea of the Church. It is probably true that, just as St. Thomas was more original and creative in ethic than dogma, so he can be said to be more original in his pneumatologico-moral notion of the Church than in his christological. In fact, what possesses remarkable power, depth and precision concerning Christ and his meaning and relevance for the Church is common to the great scholastics of the thirteenth century and reaches St. Thomas largely via St. Augustine, Hugh of Saint Victor and William of Auxerre, to say nothing of the Fathers, the Greek Fathers in particular, whose doctrine this view gathers up and presents.

Like the Fathers, St. Thomas himself had a most powerful sense of the Church's inclusion in Christ and of the immanence of Christ in the Church, a sense of the ecclesiological reality of Christ and of the christological reality of the Church.

Ecclesiological reality of Christ. When God became flesh, the divine-human being that He constituted, the humanity which, in Him, was joined to God *in persona*, became the head of all creation. St. Thomas saw deeply and clearly into the consequences that follow on this unique dignity. First, in the soul of Christ there was the fullness of all grace, a fullness "intensive" as well as "extensive", qualitative as well as quantitative, embracing all we can attribute to a man of the created grace of God, whether sanctifying grace with the virtues and gifts flowing from it or graces *gratis datae*. Thus, in the world of grace a kind of Platonism is valid for Christ contains in Himself the fullness of the species grace, in a way similar to that in which the archetype of Man, in Plato, contains the fullness of the human species. So that if other individuals are to receive grace too, they may only do so in dependence on Christ and, if these be men whose unique Saviour is the God-given Christ, they may only receive it from Christ and in virtue of sharing, participating, in His own grace.

St. Thomas has developed this thesis in questions 7 and 8 of the *Tertia Pars*, on the grace of Christ precisely as it is proper to Him and comes to Him as *Caput Ecclesiae*—basic questions in his ecclesiology. The following are the dominant ideas. Christ is head of the new humanity we have seen receiving from God this Godward life, which has as its goal the objects of the divine life, and which returns to the heart of the Father. Christ is the principle and head of this new economy of things, somewhat as Adam was of the first. He contains in Himself all the effects of grace which are to be later spread abroad in the Church, as the white flame enfolds all the brilliancies of colour analyzable into the spectrum. Hence St. Thomas goes so far as to say that Christ plus the Church do not make more than Christ alone, in the same way as God plus the world, which emanates from God and realizes in plurality what is one and simple in Him, do not make more than God alone. For as the world is what it is only by participation in God, thus receiving from Him but adding nothing, so the Church, new life of humanity moving Godwards, is what she is only by participation in Christ, receiving from Him, yet adding nothing. St. Thomas further says that the return of humanity to God whence we came out and whose image we bear—this return of created realities and good, *naturales bonitates quas Deus creaturis influit*—operates twice: once in Christ, for, says St. Thomas, when human nature, in which is concentrated and recapitulated all creation, was united to God in Him, *omnia flumina naturalium ad suum principium reflexa redierunt*; a second time, not in the mystery of the Incarnation itself, but in its harvest, the riches of God, humanized in Christ, scattered over all humanity so that they may return once more to their source and principle.

Thus, for St. Thomas the very structure of the Church of Christ as God-Man is radically ecclesiological, for Christ bears in Himself the whole economy of the new life, the whole of humanity reborn moving back to God, and the Church, which is the same thing, is really a kind of overflow of a fountain, or an unfolding and development of what was from the beginning realized in Christ.

CHRISTOLOGICAL RELEVANCE OF THE CHURCH. This is just the counterpart of what has been said. Nothing exists in the economy of return to God that does not spring from Christ, that is not caused by Him and first known and willed by Him, that has not in Him its pattern and is not a likeness to His perfection as image of the Father. All we do in the economy of the new creation, which is the Church, is not wrought in us except it come from Christ—"Virtue is gone out of me"—nor except it be willed and caused by Christ. And that is why it is truly the life of the Alone, *His* life, that is lived in the new humanity and quickens the Church. In truth, the whole of the *Secunda Pars*, the whole of the theological and moral life that is the new life borne Godwards, is the life of Christ in us.

The plan and the scientific process of analysis followed by St. Thomas in the *Summa* and the *Compendium Theologiae* is not exactly adapted to manifest this truth inevitably and this is undoubtedly a weakness in a plan otherwise finely conceived and vigorously applied. But there is no shadow of doubt that, for St. Thomas, the supernatural life in its entirety, theological and moral, is in use intimately as something "Christic" and sacramental and, when examined closely, there are several indications in the very structure of the *Summa* which force it to give up this secret. Let us examine just one, which seems to have outstanding importance. In the anthropological treatise which is part of the *Prima Pars, De Deo et de processu creaturarum a Deo,* St. Thomas contemplates man precisely as made in the image and likeness of God. It is of such a man—man carrying about with him and realizing the image of God—that St. Thomas speaks as a theologian. Man bearing it and realizing it, I have said, for this image is not some sort of mere statically possessed and imposed imprint; it involves a dynamic tendency towards the Object to which we are thereby likened, and it only truly realizes itself in action and movement, and the more so in proportion as the action and movement are true and perfect. That is why, in question 93, article 4, of the *Prima Pars,* St. Thomas distinguishes three degrees according to which the image of God may be realized in us, according to the more or less actually alive relation to Him, as Object of knowledge (acquaintance with) and of love, namely: (1) in potency, through the natural powers of the *mens*; (2) habitually and imperfectly, through grace; (3) actually and perfectly, in our actions and through the heavenly glory. The whole movement of the *Secunda Pars,* the entire *reditus creaturae rationalis in Deum*, is a realization of the *transire in imaginem* of which the medieval mystics speak. I am not reading into St. Thomas what may not be there. I am merely translating him, for listen to the words in which, in the prologue to the *Secunda Pars,* he prefaces the study of this *reditus in Deum*: "Since, according to St. John Damascene, man is said to be made in the image of God inasmuch as he is endowed with a spiritual power of knowledge and with free will, and is master of his actions, therefore, after treating of the exemplar, God, and the created beings emanating from his power and will, it remains to consider his image, man, precisely inasmuch as man is the principle of his actions, and has over them free disposal and dominion".

Moreover—and here is what I am trying to lead up to—the three degrees which St. Thomas, at the end of the *Prima Pars,* distinguished within the process of realization of the image of God, and of the growth in likeness to God, find their exact counterparts in the degrees of belonging to Christ and likening unto Christ which St. Thomas analyzed in an article of the *Tertia Pars, Utrum Christus sit caput omnium hominum.* I think one would hardly depart from the thought of St. Thomas in saying that the degrees of realization of the image of God, the analysis of whose richness and manifold phases is the work of the

Secunda Pars, are correlatively degrees of incorporation into Christ, degrees also of conformity, of likening and assimilation to Christ: for He is emphatically, in the terms of the prologue to the *Tertia Pars, Viam per quam ad beatitudinem immortalis vitae resurgendo pervenire possimus,* and He is this in virtue of all the things *quae per ipsum sunt acta et passa.* Whence arises St. Thomas' insistence in the *Tertia Pars* on the virtues of Christ and all He achieved and suffered in the flesh, during the time of His sojourning among us. These things are what make His life redemptive, meritorious, efficacious. These are the things whereby He is set up as our exemplar and pattern to be contemplated as the measure and standard of our own fashioning, becoming like unto Him in the movement of our return towards God, the return analyzed in the *Secunda Pars* and filled in and completed by the *Tertia Pars* in those elements which explain the birth and growth of the Church, the new creation that is in Christ Jesus.

* * *

In this way we see how the two aspects so far delineated, the one pneumatological, ethical or theocentric, the other christological, cannot be mutually exclusive, but, on the contrary, work one within the other, interpenetratively and complementarily.

All graces come, as from their first and proper cause, from God, and from God the Holy Ghost by "appropriation"; our fashioning is in the likeness of God, of His Holy Trinity, the heart of which is our end and goal and the work of the same God in us; because a work of love, it is in a special sense said to be the work of the Holy Spirit and it likens us to Him. How then can there be community of attribution between Christ and the Holy Ghost, and how is the Church the Body of Christ and not that of the Holy Spirit? Because none of these things comes to us except by Christ and in Christ—by which is meant Christ-the-Man—*qui est nobis via tendendi in Deum.* Further, since the Holy Ghost, according to St. Thomas at any rate, has, in the giving of grace and the work of our likening ourselves to God's image, no kind of proper and particular causality but appears as the object only of an "appropriation", Christ, in His humanity joined to the divinity *in persona*, has a true and particular causality, though instrumental. St. Thomas revives a teaching of the Greek Fathers, especially St. Cyril of Alexandria and St. John Damascene, when he calls Christ the organ, the conjoined instrument, having its causality in the giving; a living instrument, having its initiative, while entering the situation by human knowledge and human will, the knowledge and the will of Priest-King-Saviour. Moreover Christ, in His gracious humanity, humanizes the divine life communicated; He is truly able to be *Head* of the Church and the Church really His Body, because He is homogeneous with it through His human nature. In it, Christ is become a member and individual among the general concourse of humanity and therefore He can rise to be its Head so that it becomes His Body.

In this manner the newness of human life coming back to God is shared between the Holy Ghost and Christ; the newness of life called the Church: God—by "appropriation" God the Holy Ghost—is the end and active power of this divine life. Ultimately all things come from Him and we are made more and more like unto Him, living by the things and ends which make up His own divine life.

Christ, in His holy and gracious humanity, is properly the instrumental cause, besides being an intelligent and voluntary cause, of the gifts of God; and, on the plane of exemplary and final causality, He offers to us a divine life humanized and fitted to our condition of saved children of wrath. It is first to Him, and then, in Him and through Him to God, that we are fashioned and moulded, living first with Him and in Him the things ineffable of His life of redeeming and saving Sonship before the Father.

* * *

What we have seen so far defines for us the profoundest characteristic of St. Thomas' idea of the Church, with its triple phase: pneumatological, anthropological or moral, and christological. The Church so conceived corresponds, as we saw, to the definition: *Congregatio hominum Fidelium*. Such a notion leads

St. Thomas, in line with the universal Latin tradition since Augustine, to consider the Church substantially one and unbroken in its movement through time—*a justo Abel usque ad finem saeculi*—an idea which assuredly does not square well with the ecclesiology of those for whom the *De Regimine Christiano* of James of Viterbo is literally "the first treatise on the Church"; yet I repeat that it is universal among the ancient writers of the West since the golden age of the patristic period.

Meanwhile it would not be accurate to conclude that the ancient writers, including St. Thomas, stopped there and remained silent concerning those things which are studied and defended in the separate treatises "De Ecclesia" today—distinctive marks, organization in the form of a kingdom, the authority that rules it. Indeed, discussions of elements of the Church which are more external find plenty of room in St. Thomas and are clearly and strongly marked. St. Thomas had a doctrine on the powers of the Church, on the Priesthood, jurisdiction, the constitution of the Church, the Papacy and the Episcopate, on the magisterium of the Church, the relations of Church and State, of the spiritual and the temporal; he has even a sketch of the "properties" of the Church, which ultimately, after many vicissitudes, became the apologetical notes.

Since there is not space to discuss these elements at length, let us try rather to throw into relief the thought which binds them with the elements already discussed. The Institutional-Church or Social-Church appears in St. Thomas as something most closely bound up with the Church as Mystical Body, as new life in Christ through the Holy Ghost, which we have already examined as his first and deepest idea concerning the Church. This intimate fusion of the inward unity and the elements of the outward unity seems to be manifested in St. Thomas through two chief ideas: (1) the Church-as-Institution is the very mode of being of the Mystical Body and of the new life in Christ; (2) she is the Sacrament of the ministry, that is, the instrument of realization of the Mystical Body.

THE CHURCH-AS-INSTITUTION IS THE VERY MODE OF BEING OF THE MYSTICAL BODY AND OF THE NEW LIFE IN CHRIST. It is most important to note that St. Thomas does not separate the visible and the invisible, interior and spiritual elements in the Church. If we recall the text of his commentary on the Creed, with which we began, it is interesting to see how "the Angelic Doctrine unites and fuses into one whole all the visible and invisible elements, how he sets the Holy Ghost, grace and sanctity, virtues, communion of saints, in the constituted Body, the society established by Christ, propagated by the Apostles, spread abroad in the world, united in the Pope of Rome . . . how he traces back to Abel this same society which he holds to be founded by Christ and the Apostles"; if we refer to the article of the *Secunda Secundae*, q. 39, a. 1, on Schism, it is seen how St. Thomas passes quite naturally from the sin of schism defined in relation to Christ and the spiritual unity of the Mystical Body, to the sin of schism defined in relation to the inward unity of the Church-as-social-organism and in relation to the Pope, its visible leader.

This is because, for St. Thomas, the Church is its outward unity—Church as society—in other words as an organization of mutual help or co-operation under a hierarchical authority, is not a different reality from the living Body of new life in Christ, whose soul is the living Spirit, the Holy Ghost. The latter is the inward mode of that which appears outwardly as a community organized and ruled by the Hierarchy.

Doubtless St. Thomas is well aware that certain facts and problems imply a distinction between the mode of the Mystical Body as such and the mode of social manifestation of the Institutional Church. He realizes that the hierarchy of sanctity and union with Christ does not necessarily correspond to the social hierarchy of sacred ministries; he knows that one can be within the visible unity of the Church and at the same time have lost the life of sanctifying grace and even one's very faith, and that on the other hand a soul can be inwardly justified and have the grace of living faith without being in visible union with the Church—in the first case one is in the Church *numero tantum, et non merito,* in the second case, *voto*. Yet these distinctions only affect individual souls, not the Church herself. A given individual can belong to the Church in a hidden manner unknown even to himself, but that in no way leads to the conclusion that the Church herself is purely spiritual or indefinable. Rather does that individual belong invisibly to the one Church, which is at once visible and spiritual; and similarly for the other cases. The Church embraces spiritual and invisible, institutional and visible elements, but for St. Thomas there is only one Church whose inward being manifests itself in an organic society, whose outward veil contains for the soul the spiritual realities of grace, above all the Holy Spirit: "*Ecclesia catholica est unum corpus. . . . Anima autem quae hoc corpus vivificat est Spiritus Sanctus*".

Touching upon many elements of the tradition and experienced life of the Church, St. Thomas has in different places in his work a very profound and fairly developed theology of the Church as an organized Body. On the one hand, his sociological work provides us with all the elements of a theology of the Church as society, of a theology of the differentiation of function in view of a common good in which consists that *ens sociale* applied suggestively by St. Thomas himself to the Church. He does so in one of his short clear formulae to which the greatest developments do not seem to add much: "*Est in Ecclesia invenire ordinis unitatem secundum quod membra Ecclesiae sibi invicem deserviunt et ordinantur in Deum*". On the other hand, at the end of the *Secunda Pars* where St. Thomas, after analyzing fully the obligations common to all men, goes on to study what differentiates them, namely the Charismata, the active and contemplative "lives", and the states of perfection, we will find rich elements for a theology of the Church as a society differentiated and established under a hierarchy: a theology whose general idea is suggested by the second article of question 183, *Utrum in Ecclesia debeat esse diversitas officiorum seu statuum*. Its teaching is repeatedly echoed, for example:

> The diversity of states and functions in the Church is conditioned by three things: the perfection of the Church, according to the same law which holds already in the sphere of natural creation that what exists modally simple and in God is participated and reproduced in the multiple and diverse fashion in creatures; secondly, by the need of differentiation of functions; thirdly, by the nobility and beauty of the Church, which consists of a certain "order". This diversity of functions does not vitiate the unity of the Church, for this unity finds its perfection in the unity of faith, love, and service, in that bond among members who strengthen one another, of which the Apostle speaks. . . . The diversity of functions works peace and unity in so far as many thus share in one action. As the Apostle says again: That there be no division in the Body, but that the members be solicitous one for another.

THE CHURCH-AS-INSTITUTION IS THE SACRAMENT, THE MINISTRY, IN SHORT, THE INSTRUMENT OF REALIZATION OF THE MYSTICAL BODY. The Church is realized as a Body living in and through men who become the recipients of the treasure of heavenly light and grace, of salvation and newness of life circulating in the whole Christ our Saviour, to the life-giving Cross. This is achieved, says St. Thomas, by faith and the sacraments of faith: by faith first, because the rebirth is of the soul, the personality, and is rebirth through a spiritual force with which we are to be bound by a spiritual contact. The sacraments, in various ways, bring to us, beneath a sensible form called for by our nature and the Incarnation which itself follows the logic of our nature, the redeeming and life-giving power of the Cross; but, among the sacraments, there is one which contains in itself and gives purpose and significance to all the others; this is the sacrament of the Holy Eucharist in which the redeeming Body and Blood of Christ are really present. Wherefore it substantially contains, says St. Thomas, the common spiritual good of the whole Church.

Thus we see why St. Thomas describes the Church as constituted, moulded, founded and blessed by faith and the sacraments of faith. We see also why he tells us that the Church was born on Calvary, appearing under the form of water and blood, *ex latere Christi formata*, formed of the dead Christ sleeping in death, like Eve formed from the side of the sleeping Adam. It would be easy to illustrate this traditional teaching from iconography.

The Church certainly appears here in a new light, as comprising the elements that complete the preceding. She is now no longer the Body of Christ simply, but also the means of realization and construction of that Body; she is the Mother and, so to say, the matrix, the ground of a new world in which Christians subsist, live and move and have their being. She contains the means of begetting them, of nourishing them, and of making them grow and flourish in Christ, as members of His Body, the Body that is herself in the mode of her underlying substance. And these means which are gathered under two heads, faith and the sacraments of faith, the Church herself as economy of realization of the Body of Christ, Church-as-Institution, is, in fact, definable in terms of those two things: faith and the sacraments of faith. The Church visible, the Church institutional, is the ministry of faith and of the sacraments of faith, by which men are grafted into Christ and realize the Mystical Body which is the Church in its inward substance. We touch here the second definition of the Church given by St. Thomas which relates to it, not only in its spiritual substance, identical from Abel to the end of the world, but in its condition of society founded by Christ: *Ecclesia, id est fides et fidei sacramenta.*

The Church in its institutional and visible reality, in that aspect which has become the subject of a separate treatise, appeared to St. Thomas as defined and constituted by the ministry of faith and the sacraments of faith and in terms of its goal—for the Eucharist is the final cause of all else—by the ministry of the redeeming Blood. All things, for him, derive from it. It is because she holds the ministry of the true Body of Christ that the Church has power over the Mystical Body. This power over the Mystical Body involves principally the power to purify and enlighten souls by the preaching of the truth and that of preparing or disposing for the reception of the Eucharist by a juridical control: in the internal forum by the exercise of the power of the keys, in the external forum by the rule of the spiritual power. St. Thomas asserts that all such powers over souls come to the Church solely from the power or ministry which she has in the celebration of the Eucharist, the sacrament of Christ Crucified, sacrament of our salvation.

Thus her whole ministry consists, whether in the celebration of the Eucharist or in exercising functions that spring therefrom and are preparatory to it, in applying to each soul, across the centuries, the universal cause of salvation and of life found and given by Christ in His Passion. In short, the Church-as-Institution is the sacrament of the Cross, the sacrament of the unique mediatorship of Christ Crucified. Again she is the sacrament, the effective sign and giver of the gift of new life and of union of men in Christ their Saviour. This mystery St. Thomas studies in detail in the *Tertia Pars, De ipso Salvatore, de Sacramentis ejus quibus salutem consequimur* (prol.).

We can now understand the literalness, the realism, and depth of this doctrine, itself part of the common tradition of Catholic theology since Augustine. The unity of the Mystical Body is the reality attained by that sacrament which is the source, the end, the beginning and the consummation, of all the others, that by which and for which the Church is made—the Church the mystery of faith, of which we are speaking, as well as the material building—namely the Eucharist. In numerous texts St. Thomas asserts that the *Res hujus Sacramenti*, that is, the thing attained by the effective symbolism of the sacrament, is the *Unitas corporis mystici*.

I cannot here further develop this doctrine with all its incidentals and consequences; but I want only to note its general relevance to the "treatise on the Church" of St. Thomas, or rather the treatise which could be written with the guidance of his principles. The whole Church is a great sacrament, whose soul is the Eucharist, whence flow and whither tend all the other sacraments and sacramentals, powers and ministries. This sacrament considered outwardly is, as it were, a *Sacramentum tantum*: the Institution with its rites, organization, hierarchy, law. But the sacrament embraces both *Sacramentum et Res*, the thing which it is really made to produce or attain as its spiritual effect: in the Eucharist the outward rite signifies and attains the real presence of Christ beneath its *species*. This *Res et Sacramentum* in turn is the sign and principle of attainment of a pure, inward reality of grace, the *Res tantum*. In the likeness of the Eucharist and by the power of its grace the Church-as-Institution, considered as a great sacrament, attains this *Unitas corporis mystici*. This last consists of faith and supernatural love in the life of living faith. What the sacraments attain effectively, the action of the spiritual rule seeks ministerially in its own way. St. Thomas puts it in a singularly striking way, both in his treatise on the new law, where he insists that all the directions of this law are "*dispositiva ad gratiam Spiritus Sancti*"—and this holds for *everything* in the Church-as-Institution, laws, rites, even rubrics, etc.—and also in the *Contra errores Graecorum*, where he describes the role of the Pope which is to subject the Church to the inward action of Christ which, through His Holy Spirit, consecrates to Him His Church, impressing upon it His seal and image—and this, again, affects the entire spiritual rule of the hierarchy.

Here we find that we have returned to our starting point: whether in its pneumatologic and moral, christologic, or institutional and sacramental, phases the Church is for St. Thomas a new life of humanity, the divine life led by men when they receive for their contemplation and goal the objects of the life of God. They are received in faith and in love.

* * *

The ecclesiological thought of St. Thomas is so rich and there are in his work so many ecclesiological elements that, to fulfil our aim of studying his idea of the Church, a whole treatise on the Church would have to be written.

But it can hardly be too strongly emphasised that this treatise would be rather different from the more or less derivative treatises of the *De Regimine Christiano* of James of Viterbo and of the controversies of Bellarmine. In reality everything in the thought of St. Thomas has an ecclesiological phase and the author of an essay on his theology of the Mystical Body has gone so far as to say that this doctrine is the heart of his theology. The reason is that the Church is not a separate reality, something outside the Christian-Trinitarian mystery, outside the anthropologic, christologic, sacramental thing which is the subject of theology. So much is this true, that I am forced to ask myself if it be not a deliberate act on St. Thomas' part that he has refused to write a *separate* treatise *De Ecclesia,* seeing that the Church pervaded his theology in all its parts. I am indeed inclined, personally, to think so. In any case, it must be obvious that, if we are going to make up a treatise *De Ecclesia,* we must use for its making both theological as well as other elements, canonical, juridical, or sociological; and not just these without the first. While completing the more mystical doctrine of the middle ages by the study of other elements more strongly brought out subsequently, we must not neglect the element which we have termed ecclesiological. It must be sought and separated—from the Trinity, the Divine *Missiones,* anthropology and ethic, christology and soteriology, sacraments and hierarchic ministry. So we shall preserve purely, as St. Thomas did, the full, large and undefiled Catholic tradition, the inspiration of the Fathers. That tradition can be characterized by three marks: the Church is contemplated as a Spirit-moved, Spirit-known and Spirit-defined reality, as the Body whose living Soul is the Spirit of Life. The Church is contemplated in Christ, as Christ is contemplated in the Church. And the inward Church is not separated from the outward Church, which is its sacramental veil and vehicle. I think no one will deny this to be the ecclesiology of the Fathers. And I hope that I may have proved it to be that of St. Thomas Aquinas.

IV

The Mystical Body of Christ

THE PRESENT SHORT STUDY does not claim to present a complete theory of the Mystical Body such as a formal theological treatise would require. All it sets out to do is, from the point of view of the spiritual life of the ordinary Christian, to state what the Mystical Body actually is and what its realization demands of us. This will be treated of under the following heads:

(1) A life led in the name of Christ.
(2) By faith.
(3) By charity.
(4) Union with the mystery of Christ by the sacraments.
(5) That he may be all in all.

* * *

(1) *A life led in the name of Christ*

"I am alive; or rather, not I; it is Christ that lives in me" (Gal. ii. 20).

Everything is contained in this. The Mystical Body is realized once our life belongs to Christ. Then it is that we lead, in this life, a life which is his, his life in us, his life in humanity; then it is that we are truly his members.

We are sinners and Christ is the holy one of God. As sinners, we are exiled far from the face of God; but we regain access to him in Christ and the Father can no longer refuse to hear and receive us when we appear before him bearing, as it were, the features and clothed with the justice of Him in whom he has placed all his delight, like Jacob presenting himself to Isaac for his blessing with the features of his elder brother and clothed with his garments.

If the Father has really placed all his delight in Christ, we can please him only if he sees us in Christ, if, in truth, we are in Christ, if we do not present ourselves before him outside of Christ, but rather as if immersed in his shadow, treading in his footsteps—better still, as members of his Body.

If, in truth, "no one has ever gone up into heaven, but there is one who has come down from heaven, the Son of Man who dwells in heaven" (John iii. 13), it is clear that we can gain access to God only in the Son who, ever at the side of the Father, was made man and sacrificed himself in order to take us with him; he is the one door of the sheepfold (John i. 1).

Sinners as we are, we can only regain God in Christ.

In this, however, all the initiative belongs to him. It is not so much we who appropriate his holiness or mimic him in his life of sonship; it is rather he who, having come for our sakes, continues in mankind the act of love and praise of the Father which he performed first on this earth as both God and one of us, in the name of us all; it is he who, "having become man that we might become God", works not only his own Incarnation, but our divinisation. It is, in truth, a divine life he gives us to lead in the body through his grace; the power of the Holy Spirit is not confined to the generation of Christ in Mary's womb, but also is what generates Christians in the womb of the Church.

What Christ asks of us for this purpose is to open our souls to him, to deliver our lives up to him and to put ourselves entirely at his disposition, so that we no longer live our own life on our own account exclusively but that, by his grace, we live his own life and on his account.

A Christian, in fact, is one who, though in a body subject to death, lives not merely the life of the flesh but the holy and pure life of Christ; one whose actions proceed not from a human source, from flesh and blood, but from Christ; one who constantly refers himself to the standpoint and desires of another. He has made himself over to this other, and his whole desire is to decrease that he may increase. The real animating principle of his life, the real spring and motive of all he does, are not his own opinion and will but those of another whom he has made the master of his destiny.

It is not simply a question of a moral consecration of our life to Christ and of a greater or lesser fidelity to his inspiration, but our acts are to be considered as his own and they must be so in fact. The new life so entered upon must be truly his life, and this all springs from the fact that he has regenerated us by his grace, that we are truly reborn by water and the spirit. Thus, it is not just a moral life on the human plane inspired by Christ but actually a life of Christ in mankind.

Since we belong to him in this way and he vivifies us, we are truly his members. Since all who are given over to him in one and the same way receive a new life, which is his life, from one and the same source, which is his Spirit, we are all together and equally his Body and his Church—the possessive pronouns must be taken in the original and full sense they have in St. Paul.

The Mystical Body is realized in practice when we come to lead our life on Christ's account.

* * *

One practical consequence follows immediately, that there is no possibility of a Christian life unless the natural man renounces himself. Since it is a question of causing another to live in me, I must first of all renounce my absolute autonomy.

This initial consent to the invasion of my life by another must be renewed every day and in all things. We must accept that another feeds on our own substance and grows in us, or rather desire that we should grow in him and feed our life on his. All through this growth of Christ in me or of me in Christ it is the case that he who loses his life finds it, and he who tries to keep it loses it. Loss and gain are divinely intermingled and strictly proportional, a *quotidie morior* allowing a progressive *vivit vero in me Christus*, the inward man growing by what the outward man loses (2 Cor. iv. 6). On the one hand, it is certainly our human substance that is consumed by Him who, lifted up from the earth, draws all things to himself, and so we lose our life. On the other, we gain all in him, the joy of increasing advance, unity with our brethren, the kingdom of God with all the rest given with it; and, in this way, we save our life.

Pastoral experience is quite definite on this point, that souls are divided into those that are open and those that are closed. If it is a question of coming to faith from a state of unbelief, there are those who at least accept to run the risk of belief; they are open to the demands of faith ("Who is he, Lord, that I may believe in him?"). And there are others who remain enclosed in the finicky and placid limitations of their contemptible egoism, whatever be the disinterested motive they adduce to justify their barren existence.

If it is a question of progress in the Christian life, there are, too, men of desire who never consider themselves to have arrived ("non quod jam perfectus sim . . ."), but wish always to grow further and, to that end, open themselves more and more to Christ's call and his demands. And there are those who soon come to think they have done enough and who settle down, become hardened, take all kinds of precautions and are soon well inoculated against any excess of divine love.

It is only too true that souls are divided according as they are open or closed; the former are ready to receive the life of Christ, the latter are unwilling to risk sacrificing theirs to him. That is why Our Lord says that the harlots may well enter the kingdom of heaven before those ostensibly just. For if we are satisfied with ourselves, shut up and placid in our sufficiency, if we think ourselves very well as we are, just and wise in quite an adequate degree, we, in fact, have no need of anything and he who came only for those who were sick will have nothing to give us. "I find thee neither cold nor hot, I would thou wert one or the other. Being what thou art, lukewarm, neither cold nor hot, thou wilt make me vomit thee out of my mouth" (Apoc. iii. 15–16). But if we are poor and acknowledge ourselves sinners, if we call on him for mercy, Christ is able to heal and enrich us.

That void from which we call on him he will fill with himself. There where we admit ourselves not to be, in the desire that he will come, he is present already, living and risen; he takes over the leadership when we decline it. Let us pray, then, with the early Christians (*Didache* x. 6): "Let grace come and the world pass away. . . . Maran Atha! Come, Lord Jesus".

(2) *By Faith*

"Faith which is the flesh of the Lord" (Ignatius, *Trall.* viii. 1).

We have to hand over our life to Christ, to live on Christ's account so that he may live his life in us and realize, with us, his Mystical Body. Now it is by faith that we open up and deliver our lives to Christ and that his life begins to develop in us. Consequently, the first commitment we embark upon when we are brought to baptism in order to be made members of Christ is expressed in the following dialogue:

"What do you ask?"

"Faith".

"What does faith bring to you?"

"Eternal life".

What, then, does belief consist in? It is to accept Christ's way of viewing things, no longer assessing life and the rest from the natural, human point of view but trying to see them from that of Christ and according to the Christian scale of values. To the world, this life alone matters; to faith, all we do here is related to another life which we prepare and begin now and this earth is no abiding place, but a way.

Belief means casting the net where we have caught nothing the whole night long, if, at dawn, the Lord bids us do so. It is to play our part, commit our whole life, on Christ's word. It is to say "yes" to God, to accept his conditions, to entrust him with the direction of our life, to hand him the key of our soul—"I have taken Christ for my Master for ever" (R. Bazin). It is to embrace the views of God, to judge things as he judges them, from a divine and Christian standpoint.

From this it can be seen how faith initiates and continues the realization of the Mystical Body. For if being a member of the Mystical Body means to lead our life on Christ's account and to live on this earth his own life, this all begins when we abandon our human point of view to adopt that of God and to conform our own view, as far as we can, to his vision of things.

Prayer, the exercise of faith, is, obviously, where we steep ourselves most thoroughly in God's view; it is in prayer that we can best adjust our view to that of our Father in heaven, by imitating the model, fraternal to us and filial to God, given by the incarnate Word, Jesus Christ. The perfect prayer he taught us is summed up in the will that all should be done on earth as in heaven, for that is to embrace the views of God absolutely. All true prayer comes to that.

* * *

We must, however, go still further and pursue, at a deeper level, in the same sphere of faith, the reality of the Mystical Body. The conformity of our life to that of Christ, which is the substance of the Mystical Body, is not brought about, as we have said, so much by our own effort to reproduce Christ as by a gift of Christ continuing and prolonging himself in mankind.

Likewise, the new outlook on things which proceeds from faith is not the result of our personal efforts so much as an antecedent gift of God. The Mystical Body is, from beginning to end, a re-creation of humanity in Christ, a re-creation of humanity to the image of God. If God's first demand on us is to embrace Christ's view of things, we are not called upon to do so by a detailed imitation of a model which remains external and foreign to us, but by a gift which renews us really and internally according to this model. "See how God has shown his love towards us; that we should be counted as his sons, *should be* his sons. If the world does not recognize us, that is because it never recognized him. Beloved, we are sons of God *even now*, and what we shall be hereafter has not been made known as yet. But we know that when he comes *we shall be like him*; *we shall see him then as he is*" (1 John iii. 1–3).

The ultimate completion of this new creation in Christ, which is tantamount to our generation to the status of sons of God, is our being made like God to the point of seeing him as he is. Its first stage, an absolutely real one, though only initially so, is being like to God by learning to know him and to see things as he sees them. Since we begin here, in very real fashion, our life as sons of God, it is here already that we have a share in our Father's nature, that we become a new creature in Christ and that we receive, straightaway, the gift of a new outlook.

For that purpose, God begins the renewal of our being by grafting on to our human outlook a principle giving us a new outlook conformable to his own. He gives us, in real truth, new eyes, eyes of faith, eyes that see and illuminate, eyes that illumine what they perceive and so see things in the light of God.

Faith is an interior light derived from the light of God which illumines all things in the light of God and makes us see them as he does. It is no illumination from without, not even a power magnifying that of our human vision, but a new sight grafted on our actually existent humanity, new eyes, the eyes of the Father, source of a new gaze which is the gaze of God, since it comes from him, and which is also my gaze, since it is really engrafted and adapted in my own life.

Thus, there is in me a principle of vision and, in more general fashion, a principle of action that is strictly divine, a possibility of seeing things with the eye of God. The Christian performs acts and leads a life whose true principle is Christ; his way of seeing and judging is Christ's way; his life springs not so much from himself as from Another whose standpoint he has embraced and whose vision he has received for his own. This, surely, is the realization of the Mystical Body, of a life led on Christ's account. What fullness of meaning this gives to the words so often recurring in St. John and St. Paul—"May Christ find a dwelling-place, through faith, in your hearts" (Eph. iii. 17); "The man who listens to my words . . . has passed over already from death to life" (John v. 24, cf. iii. 15, etc.); "I am alive, or rather not I; it is Christ that lives in me. True, I am living, here and now, this mortal life; but my real life is the faith I have in the Son of God" (Gal. ii. 20).

We have all of us seen a landscape, grey, gloomy and sullen, all at once lit up by the sun's rays. The whole scene changes in a moment: the fields are gay, the various features stand out clearly, there is a general impression of gladness and fecundity.

In some such way, faith illumines everything in a new way. To the eyes of faith, which illuminate what they look at, the dull landscape of life appears in a fresh light coming from the "Father of lights". Life takes on a new meaning according to that which God gives it; all values are transformed. Instead of the maxims of the world, such as "Whoever sacrifices profit to principle is a fool", we have those of Christ given in the sermon on the mount—"Blessed are the poor in spirit", and all that is contained in chapters v to viii of the Gospel according to St. Matthew. We make our own Christ's way of looking at things; we apply ourselves to adopt his judgments of value, to let him direct our life and arrange our destiny. All our actions are done in accordance with his, for "if our eye is pure, our whole body is in the light". That is truly the realization of a life led on Christ's account; even more, it is the continuation of his life in ours, and therein lies the whole mystery of his Mystical Body.

(3) *By charity*

"Faith which is the flesh of the Lord and charity which is the blood of the Lord" (Ignatius, *Ad Trall.*, viii. 1).

Christ enters into us by faith; he lives in us by charity. Faith is God's outlook engrafted on to us; through charity, his heart beats within us. That, indeed, is saying a great deal; but why does God send his Spirit into our hearts (2 Cor. i. 22; Rom. v. 5) if such is not the case?

Some of the saints experienced this very literally. St. Catherine of Siena told her confessor that once when she pronounced with especial fervour the words of the psalm (Ps. 42), "Create in me a clean heart, O God", she saw Christ come to her, open her side and take away her heart, and, afterwards, put his own there instead. Since that time, she spoke no more of *her* heart, but of *the* heart. A like happening is recorded in the lives of a fairly considerable number of holy persons. In our own day, Fr. William Doyle, an army chaplain, killed near Ypres in 1917 while ministering to the troops, relates: "I had the conviction that Jesus was standing quite close to me. I remember saying to him, 'Fill my heart with your love'. Then I remained motionless, while Jesus (I can only express the thing in this way) took his own heart and poured its love into mine".

The physiological side of these facts has no importance at all. What they signify is that God puts in us his living love as he has put in us his living gaze so that, through charity, we may love all things as he loves them, just as, through faith, we see things as he sees them.

Charity transplants, acclimatizes and engrafts in our weak, human hearts the very motive force of God's love, tendencies conformable to God's own creative intentions. It makes us embrace God's interests and desires, makes us will what he wills, love what he loves for the motives and, so far as is possible, in the fashion he loves them. That is why charity, being conformed to the intentions of God which are sovereign and creative of their object, recovers the true meaning of the creation and alone understands God's work in souls and in the world.

In us, love is the moving power of all our other faculties; it is the soul and so the vivifier of all we do, so much so that the dominant inclination in a soul has command of its whole life and rules all its powers. For that reason, one is absolutely and completely king only by love and God alone, since he can claim absolute and total love, is fully and universally king.

In the degree to which we let charity assert itself and grow within us we have delivered our life over to God and let Christ take to himself all the living cells, the active fibres of our being. In the same degree, he is the spring of our actions, he expresses himself in whatever we do; it is he who "lives our life" (Pascal).

For this reason, those who are truly the friends of Our Lord are the most living members of his Mystical Body. For the same reason, the Mystical Body does not consist in exterior manifestations or ceremonies, however valuable or striking they be. But it is when a small child, a humble lay-sister, a working mother whose life is taken up with ordinary daily chores, when people like this, unnoticed by the world, love God with all their heart and live a life of ardent charity, then the Mystical Body is realized and increased in stature. Such persons bring about the kingdom of God and grow in holiness to the profit of all, for it is only as Christ's members that we grow in him by charity, so that the whole body benefits from the advance of each.

* * *

It belongs to the nature of charity, then, that it is not only union with God, but communion with men. Indeed, it is when we love God, are joined to him by charity and embrace his own loving intentions that we are able to love ourselves, to love others and all good things with a love free from self-seeking.

God's own sovereign love, since it exists prior to the goodness of what it loves and actually creates it, is alone perfectly disinterested and alone merits the name of love, But, when we love with God's own love sent into our hearts by the Holy Spirit, we love from a motive above and beyond our selfish and personal interests; we love with a love whose motive and source transcend even the distinction between *another* and *myself*. It is by charity alone that we are able, in absolute truth, to love others as ourselves, without thereby in the least infringing our own good. That is because, where charity is concerned, there is no longer a neighbour who is really other than me and alien. If I love with the heart of God, my love proceeds from a source where there is no question of myself and another, but of the Father, of Christ, and of the members of his Body; it is an image of the love Christ himself bears for his Church. Strictly speaking, it is no longer a matter of another person, but of members of a single body. When St. Paul calls on us to "be followers of God, as most dear children" and to "walk in love as Christ also hath loved us" (Eph. v. 1–2), he goes on to explain that "no man ever hated his own flesh, but nourisheth and cherisheth it, as also Christ doeth the Church, because we are members of his Body" (Eph. v. 29).

It is from the same realistic outlook that we are to understand the "as oneself", the mode of loving of true charity; it would take too long to work this out in detail. This is how St. Augustine characterizes charity: "It does not seek its own interests; it puts the good of all before its own good, and not its own before that of all". St. Paul tells us that, if we bear one another's burdens, we fulfil the law of Christ (Gal. vi. 2). Our Lord himself sums it all up in these words: "'You have heard that it was said, Thou shalt love thy neighbour and hate thy enemy. But I tell you, Love your enemies, do good to those who hate you, pray for those who persecute and insult you, that so you may be true sons of your Father in heaven, who makes his sun rise on the evil and equally on the good, his rain fall on the just and equally on the unjust. If you love those who love you, what title have you to reward? Will not the publicans do as much? If you greet none but your brethren, what are you doing more than others? Will not the very heathen do as much? But you are to be perfect, as your heavenly Father is perfect'" (Mt. v. 43–48). There is nothing further to be said. These words say all and are to be taken absolutely literally.

* * *

This communion, brought into being by charity, which unites men in the very degree in which they are united to God, is, undoubtedly, what constitutes the Mystical Body. Charity makes Christ live in us and unites us, one to the other, all together, in God.

But we can go even further than this. If we form a single body and, as it were, a single being who loves in Christ, that is so ultimately, because we are all interiorly animated by one and the same soul; and, at a deeper level still, because the same charity, animating the whole body, is spread abroad in it and upheld by a single living Being who is the Spirit of Christ, the ultimate principle of the unity of the Mystical Body—"one body and one Spirit" (Eph. iv. 4).

(4) *We are united to the mystery of Christ by the Sacraments*

"There is only one mediator between God and men, Jesus Christ, who is a man, like them, and gave himself as a ransom for them all" (St. Paul, 1 Tim. ii. 5).

The idea of the Mystical Body we have set forth up to this point may well seem inadequate. We have spoken mainly of a life of dependence on Christ, led on Christ's account, according to the views and intentions of God. It may seem as if it was a question of a highly moral kind of human life belonging to Christ and drawing its inspiration from him, but belonging to him simply as an external thing in his possession and inspired by him as a master or a model seen more or less from a distance.

But there is much more than that. Clement of Alexandria's Christ-teacher would not be the Christ of the Mystical Body if St. Cyril had not gone on to affirm an interior, vivifying, sanctifying Christ, imparting his own life to the whole of humanity. Indeed, the Mystical Body is not only humanity consecrating itself to God and imitating Christ, but humanity living the life of Christ or, what comes to the same, Christ continuing his life in humanity. When we consecrate our life to him it is that he may fill it with his own. The life of the Mystical Body is not just a life of religion which could be his own; it is actually his own.

This is the meaning and function of the Christian sacraments. Human in their outward form, repeatable at will, of sensible and collective significance, they put us in touch, by a special efficacy attached by Christ to their symbolism, to the unique and historical fact of the Redemption; they make us sharers of the Redemption and salvation established in Christ dead and risen for us.

They are not new facts, not even, strictly speaking, new acts but, in a quite special mode of a symbolical and real, that is sacramental, celebration, the very presence, in its substance (the Eucharist), or at least in its sanctifying power (Baptism and the other sacraments), of the redemptive mystery of Christ.

All Christians are thus brought into relation with Christ himself, the very same Christ who, at a particular time, suffered under Pontius Pilate and rose from the dead. The nourishing sap that is thus assured to them is none other than that of the tree of the cross and the life animating them is the life of Christ himself. All this is the meaning and purpose of the sacraments. They are precisely the means by which is realized the unity, or rather the uniqueness, of Christ's mediation. So far from being an inducement for Christians to rely on and trust to human agency, they are but the affirmation and effective realization of the unique mediation of Christ.

Homo, Christus Jesus. Mediation of the man-Christ, for men; all in this is homogeneous with man, co-natural with him; that is to say it is both sensible and spiritual, personal and collective, interior and exterior. The sacraments, like the Church as a whole, are a prolongation of the incarnation of the Word and follow out, in their scheme and manner, the logic of its theandric character. The Holy Ghost brings about the incarnation of the Word, who is born "ex muliere"; the generation of Christians in the womb of the Church is, likewise, affected by the Holy Ghost at the same time, "ex aqua" (John iii. 5), that is to say by the means, with the co-operation and in the manner, of, a creature of sense.

The Mystical Body itself is not a reality in all respects spiritual, invisible and inapprehensible to sense. It is brought into being in intimate and organic connection with a visible Church, something institutional and social in character. The "sacrament" is the point where the two aspects meet and unite, the category wherein is expressed the necessary conjunction of the Mystical Body and the visible Church. The latter, throughout its whole being, is but the sacramentality of the unique mediation of Christ dead and risen. The subject is too vast to be exhaustively treated here, but this aspect must not be overlooked.

* * *

We do not intend either to set forth a complete doctrine of the sacraments, since we are not writing a treatise either of the Church or of the sacraments. All of these work to the building up of the Mystical Body, but far the most important are Baptism and the Eucharist and of these we must needs say something.

Baptism incorporates us with Christ and, at the same time, incardinates us in the Catholic Church. It makes us "members of the household of God and fellow-citizens with the saints" (Eph. ii. 19) and, at the same time, members of the Catholic Church, subject to the duties and acquiring the rights attached to Christian or Catholic citizenship. The latter consist of the right to the sacraments, to the benefits flowing from the Church's life and Christian mutual help and, normally, to the fullness of communion with God and the saints. The duties are, as in every other city, defined by the law, that of the Church and primarily of God, of which the first article is: "Thou shalt love the Lord, thy God, with thy whole heart and thy whole soul, with thy whole mind and all thy strength".

Above all, the baptised person becomes a living member of Jesus Christ—"we, all of us, have been baptised into a single body by the power of a single Spirit" (1 Cor. xii. 13). This truth is admirably expressed in the baptistery of St. Paul's at Geneva, where the baptismal fonts, formed by a kind of shell, are attached to the wall of a recess whose background is a mosaic by Maurice Denis representing the baptism of Christ together with a theophany of the Trinity and the various symbols of the Old Testament which prefigured baptism. The baptismal shell itself is entirely surrounded by the waters of the Jordan; the feet of the baptised Christ, immersed in the Jordan, also dip into the basin of the font. Thus, not only is the actual baptism bound up with its institution and the sacrament manifested as continuing Christ's action, but the incorporation of the infant with Christ is made, as it were, quite evident, since he who rises out of the shell in which the baptism takes place is Christ, with whom we are incorporated.

Incorporated with him is nothing else than becoming living beings animated by his life, associated to his life, placed in symbiosis with him.

The Eucharist takes us deeper still into the mystery of incorporation with Christ. There is no need to add to what Scripture plainly says; the relevant passages have a fullness of meaning which cannot possibly be mistaken: "As I live because of the Father, the living Father who has sent me, *so* he who eats me will live, in his turn, because of me" (John vi. 58). This is to be read in conjunction with the following: "That they may be one, as we are one . . . that they all may be one; that they too may be one in us, as thou, Father, art in me, and I in thee . . . that they should all be one, as we are one; that while thou art in me, I may be in them . . ." (John xvii. 11, 21, 22). "We have a cup that we bless; is not this cup we bless a participation in Christ's blood? Is not the bread we break a participation in Christ's body? The one bread makes us one body, though we are many in number; the same bread is shared by all" (1 Cor. x. 15–17).

The Eucharist is the sacrament of the redemptive mystery of the cross which it symbolizes, celebrates and makes present. It is, in addition, the sacrament of the unity of the Mystical Body, which it is its special grace to bring into being. Those are the basic facts and it is for theologians to develop their implications. It is not our intention to enter upon technical explanations at present; we hope to set them out in another work. Let these few words suffice.

In the Eucharist we receive Christ in the form of food. In consequence, according to the law of the sacraments, whose special effects result from what they signify, we unite ourselves to

Christ in a mysterious union similar to that obtaining between a living being and its food. In the natural order, the living thing assimilates its food and incorporates it into its own substance. Here, however, the roles are reversed but the effect is mysteriously alike. The Eucharist is food and it is certainly our own soul that it feeds with that incorruptible food which is Christ. But whereas, in the natural and material order, all the power of assimilation resides in us so that we reduce what we eat to form part of our own life, here the power of assimilation belongs to Christ and it is he who, in feeding us, unites us and incorporates us with his life. What Truth said to St. Augustine may be applied to the Eucharist: " 'Eat me and grow in stature. But it is not you who will change me into yourself, like bodily food, it is I who will change you into me' " (*Conf.* vii. 10).

The union with Christ which results, an infinitely mysterious one, is like the union which takes place in a living thing; it is both an incorporation and an intensification of life. For, as we have seen, Our Lord compares in the most explicit fashion the union he wishes to establish between us and himself, especially through the Eucharist, to the unity existing between him and his Father, and that is a unity of perfect life, a substantial unity of life.

What a tremendous mystery this is; especially when we compare it, in all the depth of its significance, with the slightness of the apparent and sensible effects of our communions. But the gifts of God are not to be estimated in the light of our own infidelities.

The Eucharist is, then, the perfect sacrament of our incorporation with Christ. Theologians are unanimous in holding that its special effect is to bring about the unity of the Mystical Body. By a special increase of grace and of living faith, it incorporates us with Christ precisely inasmuch as it takes us all into the supreme act of love by which he offered himself for us on the cross, "so as to bring together into one all God's children, scattered far and wide" (John xi. 52).

We cannot, then, communicate in isolation from our brethren. We communicate in the true body of Christ only by communicating at the same time in his Mystical Body; the "breaking of bread" brings with it, inseparably, the presence of Christ uniting us to himself and that of the multitude which shares in his redemption—"the one bread makes us one body, though we are many in number" (1 Cor. x. 17). There we have the whole mystery of the Mystical Body.

* * *

Thus, all the sacraments, together with the Church's whole life, itself an extension of the sacramental principle, work together to bring into being the Mystical Body, each according to its symbolism and its place in the economy of the Christian life. By their means it is truly the life of Christ that is given to us; through them we are united to the one sovereign act of salvation he executed in his "Passing to his Father"—the mystery enacted from Maundy Thursday to Easter and the Ascension.

The sacraments, besides, are the point where the institutional or visible Church and the Mystical Body meet and fuse in an organic unity. The collective, external and visible celebration of the mysteries of salvation makes salvation effectively present; the institutional Church brings about the realization of the Mystical Body, the various ministries and activities of the visible Church being ordained to "order the lives of the faithful, minister to their needs, build up the frame of Christ's body, until we all realize our common unity through faith in the Son of God, and fuller knowledge of him, and so reach perfect manhood, that maturity which is proportioned to the completed growth of Christ" (Eph. iv. 11–13).

(5) *That He may be all in all*

"Instaurare omnia in Christo" (Eph. i. 10).

What concerns us here is simple enough but of infinite significance. Christ has redeemed mankind and now man has to give glory to God. But, as we have seen, there is no one to give glory to God but Christ; he alone can go up to heaven who has come down from heaven, the Son of Man. We can only gain access to God and give glory to the Father in Christ.

It is a question, then, of giving reality "in Christ" to all the humanity redeemed by him, and that for the glory of the Father. All that is not made "in him", all that remains outside of him, is lost for the glory of God. But it is needful that nothing be lost, not the least strand of that humanity which, made to the image of God and re-created in that of Christ, is to return to its exemplar.

Our whole endeavour, then, must be, by charging them with a living faith, to realize all our sentiments, thoughts, desires, to do all our actions, "in Christ", that is to say as Christ would have done them, for his love and by his grace. We are to place all in Christ, which amounts to putting Christ in them all. Our friends must be friends in Christ; our work must be done in Christ; when we walk, eat, when we are joyful, we will do it all in Christ; that is, we will put him, by a living faith, by love, prayer and grace, in all this. We will be sad in Christ, ill in Christ, we will go to bed and get up in Christ. Above all, we are to be of service to others in Christ, pray, mortify ourselves, be patient in Christ; and so in all things our constant endeavour must be each day to leave nothing outside of him and to make all this no mere formality, but living and real.

Let us ask God to give us understanding of this. St. Patrick, the apostle of Ireland, had well grasped it when he taught his followers to sing these affirmations so full of meaning:

"Christ with me, Christ before me,
Christ behind me, Christ within me,
Christ below me, Christ above me,
Christ at my right, Christ at my left,
Christ in the fortress,
Christ seated on the chariot,
Christ on the ship's prow,
Christ in the heart of every man who thinks of me,
Christ in the mouth of every man who speaks of me,

Christ in every eye that sees me,
Christ in every ear that hears me".

Such a programme, taken in its totality, embraces absolutely the whole finality of the universe, of the Church, too, and the Redemption, which is the same, namely, to recapitulate, realize and fulfil the universe in Christ and so to render, in Christ, all glory to God. It means to bring Christ into everything till, being subjected to him, the Son himself gives homage to him who has subjected all things to him, so that God may be all in all (cf. 1 Cor. xv. 28 and Col. iii. 11).

Christ's own life on earth, his strictly personal life if we may so call it, lasted only thirty-three years. He was a child and lived at home only a few years. He taught and preached, was priest and victim. He knew joy, he worked, he commanded others.

All this which he did for our sakes he wishes to continue in us. He desires to be a child in the Christian child, to be obedient in its obedience, to live a home life in Christian parents and homes, to be joyful in those who rejoice, to continue his Passion in those who suffer. He wills to continue his teaching in those who teach, to be master in the Christian master, priest in the Christian priest, worker in the Christian worker.

In other words, we must let Christ come into each of us, into every living strand of humanity, of whatever age, state of life or condition, till he is really all in all; so that, as a result, his Mystical Body is built up, which is his Incarnation continued, the fullness of his sacred humanity consecrated to the Father; that all may be, in him, consummated in glory to God.

That is what is meant by his Mystical Body; that is the Church.

In the human body there is present a variety of functions within a unity of life. The hand takes hold, the mouth speaks and takes in food, the eye sees. All this is animated by a single soul and is attributed to the one person; it is I who take, look, talk and eat, and it is my soul that does all this through my different members or functions.

It is the same with the Mystical Body. It takes up the whole variety of human activity into the unity of a single life of holiness which is the life of Christ. It enables my actions to be attributed to Christ and finally, in a mysterious manner, makes them his, since they are the acts of his Body. It makes me into a worker of Christ, a teacher of Christ, a pupil of Christ, a priest of Christ, a housewife of Christ—"That he may be all in all".

How does this all come about? By a living faith. When, through faith animated by charity, I live for Christ, living by his grace after his manner of life, all that I do is done in him; and he, also, does in me all that I do. What St. Augustine says is true not only in the strictly sacramental order: "Peter baptises, it is Christ who baptises; Paul baptises, it is Christ who baptises . . ."; but it can be said, too, in the spiritual and moral order: "Peter takes the class, it is Christ who teaches; Paul mends tents, it is Christ who works". But, whereas, in speaking of the institutional and sacramental order, we might add, with St. Augustine: "Judas baptises, it is Christ who baptises", we cannot say likewise as regards the moral order to which the formation of the Mystical Body belongs; its very substance, in fact, is living faith and what is not done in faith, in one way or another, is not done in Christ nor may be ascribed to Christ. We cut off from his Body all that we do not give to him by living faith. Sin forms the boundary which we are constantly setting to the growth of Christ.

* * *

In Numidia, in the ruins of an ancient Christian sanctuary, has been found a clay vessel wherein had been preserved the remains of martyrs, and on whose lid were inscribed the words: "In isto vaso sancto congregabuntur membra Christi". A vivid expression of the reality of the Mystical Body.

There is no one, finally, capable of going up to heaven except him who came down from heaven, the Son of man. But, come down for us, he goes back there with us, and we go up with him. "He who so went down is no other than he who has gone up, high above all the heavens, *to fill creation with his presence*" (Eph. iv. 10).

V

The Life of the Church and Awareness of its Catholicity

THE PASSAGES of the Gospel relating to the universal mission of the apostles and of the Church will always present some difficulty to those who, accepting Christ's knowledge of the future, try to give them a consistent meaning. Harnack's own view on the universal nature of Christianity is well known. "It is historically certain", he said, "that Christ, in his lifetime, sent his disciples to preach to the Jews alone. He looked no further than the Jewish frontiers, he had in mind no other apostolate than that of his own people. It was only after his death that the words 'Go and preach' (Mt. x. 7) were taken in a Universalist sense and gave occasion to the first Christians to attribute to the risen and glorified Christ the definitive mission to 'go and teach all nations' (Mt. xxviii. 19). Matthew and Mark find no place for a mission to the pagans in the setting of Christ's public life, unless it be found in the eschatological discourse and the account of his anointing; consequently, the commandment ascribed to the risen Christ goes against all the rest of the Gospel. This order could not have come from his own lips; it is a consequence of the subsequent historical development, and only when the facts pointed to its fulfilment was it put into the mouth of the risen Christ".

We do not intend here to take up the question anew but

simply to put forward, with this problem in view, a few general considerations of a theological nature.

Whatever Christ may, in fact, have taught about the universal application of the salvation he preached, it is certainly the case that neither St. Paul in his Epistles, nor any of the apostles as reported in the Acts, ever appears to us as holding himself obliged, by any previously indicated intention of Christ's, to approach the pagans; nor, when they are criticized for so doing, do they refer to any command given by Christ when he was present with the Twelve. This much is quite certain and is remarkable enough. It has caused many critics to doubt if the expressly universalist statements recorded in our Gospels were, in fact, uttered by Christ; and to those who admit their authenticity it raises a serious problem.

What, in fact, was the justification given by those among the disciples who were reproached by their brethren for having turned to the pagans? What do the texts show as the basis which seemed to them to support directly the obligation, or at least the legitimacy, of their ministry to the Gentiles? We will follow out the narrative given in the Acts.

Up to the conversion of Cornelius, the preaching of the Gospel was confined to the spiritual boundaries of Judaism. It was the Jews and the proselytes from various countries to whom was addressed, on the day of Pentecost, the first apostolic discourse (ii. 5 and 11), and the "Greeks" mentioned in that connection (vi. 1 and 9; cf. ix. 29) were simply Greek-speaking Jews, from the same Jewish milieu as St. Paul. Now, if Peter was already aware that the call to salvation was not restricted (ii. 21 and 29; iii. 26), there is nothing to show that, at this time, his ideas went any further than those of any other Jew, and that he held that Christ's salvation transcended the religious framework of Judaism. The fact is that, at this time, the preaching of Christianity was addressed to the Jews alone (v. 31) and was, for the moment, confined to Jerusalem.

The dispersal of the brethren into Judaea and Samaria on

account of the persecution that followed Stephen's martyrdom extended the preaching of the Gospel; but it still remained within the spiritual confines and setting of Judaism and there is nothing to show that there was any idea of having to go beyond them. Saul himself, whose entire life and career was determined by the vision on the road to Damascus, does not seem to have had, at that moment, any awareness of a call to carry the name of Christ to the pagans.[1] According to the evidence of the Acts, St. Paul, though destined by God from the beginning to make Christ known to the Gentiles (Rom. i. 5), only gradually became aware of this, as he experienced the hostility of the Jews (xiii. 46–48, xviii. 6, xxviii. 25–28; cf. Rom. i. 16) and, finally, as a result of an explicit vision received in the temple at Jerusalem (Acts xxii. 17–20). In short, it was always a combination of events and of the illumination of the Holy Spirit which decided him. He himself states, in the Epistle to the Ephesians, that it was by revelation that he came to the knowledge of the "mystery" of the call of the Gentiles to salvation (iii. 3) and the "holy apostles and prophets" likewise (iii. 5); and, as to the principalities and powers of heaven, they learnt it only by seeing it carried into Christian universalism dependent on the facts and on the life of the Church animated by the Holy Ghost.[2]

As for Peter, it was quite unintentionally that, in the course of his ministry among the Jews or the Judaizers, he came into contact with the pagan world in the person of Cornelius who, for his part, was, at any rate, a sympathiser with Judaism (Acts x). What was it, in fact, that led Peter to baptise Cornelius? It was

[1] He seems, indeed, to relate his mission to announce the Gospel to the pagans to the vision on the way to Damascus (Gal. i. 16). Yet, if we look closely, the text does not say that it was at that moment that he knew what God had destined him to; he only says that it was then that God revealed his Son to him, which he did. He goes on to say "So that I could preach his Gospel among the Gentiles". In fact, in the following verses, he recounts only the acts of a ministry in countries where the influence of Judaism was prevalent.

[2] Very significant in this connection is Gal. ii. 7 sq. There we see James, Cephas and John ratify St. Paul's apostolate among the Gentiles on seeing the fact that this apostolate had been entrusted to him, and recognizing as a fact the grace given him.

the realities of the situation, as experienced by him, namely the vision of the sheet containing all kinds of animals, which decided him to go to Cornelius with the intention of following out God's indications (x. 28; 2), an event carrying its own significance, the coming of the Holy Ghost on Cornelius's family. After the vision of the sheet, Peter recognized that, though God had sent his word to the children of Israel to announce to them his salvation (x. 36), yet he takes no account of persons and grants forgiveness, in the name of Jesus, to all who believe in him. Apart from the "name of Jesus", that was no different from what a Jew might have said to a pagan to persuade him to become a proselyte; but everything is changed by reason of one fact, namely that the pagans received the Holy Ghost; therein Peter sees the finger of God and confers baptism (x. 47). It was the first time that actual pagans, however sympathetic with Judaism, received the word of God and baptism. Peter took that course for no other reason than the facts. When the "circumcised" objected, the only reply he gave was that he was led thereto by the facts (xi. 15, 17) and the objectors gave way before the fact (x. 18).

Soon the facts gained the field. At Antioch, some Christians from Cyprus and Cyrene turned their attention to the pagan, as well as the Jewish, Greeks (xi. 20), and Paul began his first mission. At the Council of Jerusalem, the question was not whether they were to preach to and baptise the Gentiles but whether the latter had to submit to the Mosaic law in order to be admitted among the brethren. Here again what decided the question, both on the part of Peter (xv. 7–11) and on that of James (xv. 14 sq.), was the fact of a so evident divine initiative itself, moreover, in perfect conformity with the prophecies.

Thus, it was in the course of becoming actually universal that the Church became aware of its universality. This conclusion is quite independent of the presence or absence of words actually uttered by Christ affirming this universality. What is certain, according to all our documents, is that the primitive Church made no appeal to any such words and that it recognized its actual call to expansion and its conditions only through the facts, by realizing such expansion and doing so under the pressure of certain events caused within itself by God. When Peter appealed to what the Lord had said (xi. 16), it was precisely to indicate that it was then that he recalled it. We might almost say that it was then that he understood what it meant, which would not be far from the truth, for in the course of the gradual discovery of its own interior law that the Church makes by living it, it is always the facts and the process of living that bring a subsequent understanding of the real significance and scope of previous experiences. When we read the 15th chapter of the Acts, we certainly have the impression that things already established for some time (namely, the possibility of the Gentiles entering the Church) only later entered properly into men's awareness. Thus, the success of the evangelisation of the pagans (xv. 3–4) brought the Church to "realize" clearly things already contained in previous declarations (ii. 39) or facts (x, xv. 7), but of whose real significance it had never become properly aware.

* * *

It seems that this is, necessarily and ordinarily, the case with all that concerns the catholicity of the Church. Catholicity is the universal capacity for unity, or the dynamic universality of the Church's principles of unity. Consequently, though unity is given straightway, catholicity, being its universality, is something potential, not, indeed, in the sense that it is quite indeterminate and could become this thing or that, but in the sense that such a property, however definite in itself, is not expressed forthwith; that is why we speak of dynamic universality. This indicates, too, the capacity inherent in the Church's principles of unity—the grace of Christ, the baptismal character, the apostolic faith, sacramental charity, community life in unity—to assimilate, fill, win over to God, reunite and bring to perfection in Christ, the whole man and all men, all human values. Such a capacity implies that every human value, while retaining its own specific character, can be "recapitulated" in Christ, that is to say revivified by his spirit (Πνεῦμα) and taken up into the unit of his Body, which is the Church. To take but one example of which it is easy to imagine others of the same kind, catholicity as the universal capacity of the Church's principles of unity means that the peculiar values of the Hindu world—values in the sphere of thought and art, values of character, language, cultural in their specific nature—can be taken up into the unity of the Body of Christ and become mystically (pneumatically), as it were, the flesh and members of the new Adam. Christ will not be complete till he has, in this way, incorporated the whole man in each of us, and all the human values lying scattered in all their variety throughout the world. For he has—and so has the Church, his Body—the capacity to bring all this together in himself unto God.

All this we know antecedently well enough, but can we say that we are really aware of the catholicity of the Church so long as we fail to grasp it in its actuality, in its actually taking up into unity of values or realities that were, at first, or seemed to be, alien to it? Constantly, the Church adopts or takes to itself, in the course of experience, things one would not have thought capable of being assimilated to its unity. Certain potentialities, hitherto ignored or unsuspected, of its principles of unity make themselves known by their exercise. The catholicity of its faith becomes the more manifest when the opportunity offers of satisfying new demands, of being received and thought out afresh by classes of persons hitherto unreached by it. The same applies to the catholicity of all the other principles of unity, that is to say of all the constitutive elements of the Church. In every sphere, the Church's potentialities are brought out by being actualised, she is brought to self-consciousness by events. That, after all, is the law of all living things.

These considerations apply equally to the future. In our view, the Church has still much to learn and to reveal about herself by growing organically through the assimilation of all the marvellous wealth and variety of human values she has not yet incorporated.

There is no doubt that, from this point of view, the three great apostolic movements of our time, Catholic Action, the work of the missions and the "ecumenical" movement (for the reunion of all dissident bodies in a single *Catholica*) offer, for the Church's theology and especially for an understanding of her catholicity, an opportunity for renewal and enrichment we must be careful not to lose.

We consider, moreover, that all this is capable of being applied still further.

It is now almost a commonplace to say that the Church arrived only by slow degrees to a precise awareness of what the primacy of the Apostolic See represents. We will confine ourselves to the aspect of the matter which recalls what we observed above in the Acts. It is well known that, as far as we can tell, the first bishop of Rome to appeal to the famous text of Matthew xvi, 18 was Callistus in his edict of indulgence (ca. 220). It is known, too, that this text was, for a long time, interpreted much less strictly than it is now and that, in any case, for many centuries, it was far from playing such a prominent role in ecclesiology as it is made to do now. Does that mean that the primacy was not, in general terms, affirmed in this text? By no means, but yet we do recognize without difficulty that its importance and full significance were only gradually perceived or, at least, expressed. We go so far as to admit that it was the facts that elucidated the meaning of the text and that the life of the institution brought out, more than anything else, the importance and the significance of its charter of foundation. It was by realizing itself that the Papacy came to understand properly and to disclose its own nature. In this sense, it is true to say with Newman that "words such as 'Thou art Peter and upon this rock I will build my Church', 'Feed my lambs', etc., are, not only commands, but prophecies and promises, promises to be interpreted by the event, by history, that is to say that of the fourth and fifth centuries, though they had received a partial fulfilment in a preceding period".[1] May we

[1] *Essay on the development of Christian doctrine* (Longmans, p. 156).

not apply to such developments and to this process of growing awareness of what the Church held within herself what St. Albert the Great says of the knowledge of faith which came into being between the Old Testament and the New, when what was believed in obscure fashion became realized, "re credita eveniente".

We might say the same of the sacraments and the relation of some of them to texts in which modern theologians see the formula of their institution, though unperceived, apparently, by earlier generations. Thus the anointing spoken of in the Epistle of St. James (v. 14–15) was solemnly defined by the Council of Trent as referring to the sacrament (Denzinger, 926, 928, 929). No doubt sacramental theology could furnish other examples in addition.

It is important to observe that all this concerns dogmas which are not pure dogmas, but also "institutions", that is to say realities given to the Church, not only as objects of faith but as something to be done, effected and practised. We are dealing here with an order of things which is not to be understood exclusively in texts and statements but comes to an understanding of itself by its own action. To it is fully applicable what Père Sertillanges so excellently says: "Authority teaches itself by its own decisions, as an intelligent grain of wheat might teach itself by watching itself grow, only dimly aware of what it bore within itself. So there is, even as regards the authority which is, indeed, the head but not the whole body, a real development, a dogmatic instruction of the Church". This consideration lies at the base of all ecclesiology. For this reason, when we apply our mind to understand such matters, it is not enough to examine the relevant texts; the Church's own life is an indispensable *locus theologicus*, as St. Thomas constantly affirms in connection with the sacraments. To confine oneself to the texts would be altogether too academic and bookish a proceeding, since the institution explains itself and comes to self-knowledge by living.

This, by no means, involves bringing back, under the cover of living developments, possibilities of heterogeneous development alien to the original formula. The institution is something definite, it has its own interior law, like any living thing and the whole course of its development is animated by the Holy Spirit. But, precisely because it is an institution and not just a dogma, more can be learned about it by watching it live than by studying its formula. The full meaning and wealth of the formula can be seen only in the light of events and facts, by the life of the institution. It is somewhat the same as with those ideas and decisions we bear within ourselves, fully formed but unconscious, which we only become aware of when, under the impact of some sudden occurrence, some circumstance or challenge, we spontaneously act in accordance with them.[1] So it is that the Church comes to a fuller understanding of her catholicity and thereby understands better the nature of her "monarchical" constitution (a most unsuitable epithet anyhow) and of the primacy it involves. She discovers both of these more clearly in the texts as she lives them. She becomes aware of the real nature and the full richness of her sacraments, of their relation to Christ and of their presence in the texts, as she makes use of them. The real content of the original formula and of the texts is brought to consciousness by the facts and we shall really know what it means for the Gospel to be preached to every creature only when that shall have been accomplished.[2]

1 These ideas are well worth following up and applying to the life of the Church and to the possession of faith *in fide Ecclesiae*. Newman alone, it seems, has made use of them in this way—See his sermon for the feast of the Purification, 1843, and his Essay on Development.

2 One writer on missiology has said that the definite commentary on the Gospels cannot be written until China, Japan and India have become Christian. Cf. Journet: "The expansion of the Church reveals her to herself" (*The Church of the Word Incarnate*, vol. 2).

VI

The Holy Spirit and the Apostolic Body, Continuators of the Work of Christ

"We have a threefold warrant in heaven, the Father, the word, and the Holy Ghost, three who are yet one" (John v. 5).

In one sense, Christ's work on earth came to an end with his "passage to his Father" (John xvii. 4); but in another sense, it still remains to be done and is to be continued by other persons than Christ himself. Thus, Christ speaks in the future tense: " 'I will come; I will see you again; I will speak; I will send you; the Father will give you another Paraclete' " (John xiv. 18; xvi. 22, 25; xv. 26 and xvi. 7; xiv. 16), " 'I will build' " (Mt. xvi. 18), etc. The messianic time is one of fulfilment, but it is also one of promise during the interval between the ascension of Christ and his second coming. This period, which is precisely the era of the Church, is characterized by a relative absence of its Head, who "must have his dwelling-place in heaven until the time when all is restored anew" (Acts iii. 21), while his body is still being formed on earth. How is Christ, in his relative absence, to build up his body or his Church? How is he to complete in us the work he accomplished only in himself in the days of his flesh? The present study aims at showing (1) that Christ formed and sent out to do his work two agents, his Spirit and his apostles; (2) that these two agents are conjoined so as to bring about together the Body of

Christ; (3) that, nevertheless, the Spirit retains a sort of liberty or autonomy, which explains one of the features of the Church's life.

(1) *Two missions. Two agents to continue the work of Christ*

When the time came for him to leave the world and his disciples, Christ arranged for the continuation of his work, the sending of his Spirit and of his apostles. This disposition of his, a kind of final testament, he made known in the discourse after the Last Supper concerning the apostles (John xiii. 16, 20; xvii. 18; concerning the Spirit, xiv. 16, 26; xv. 26). We will examine briefly both of these missions, their relations and economy.

The mission of the apostles is presented as already in being or, at any rate, as already inaugurated. In fact, the apostles had been called one by one and then collectively designated as such. Within the apostolic body, Peter had been set apart and nominated for the function of rock or foundation (Mt. xvi. 13–19). The apostles had received special instructions from the Master, together with different powers to exercise over the future flock of believers in Christ (e.g. Luke ix, 1 sq.; Mt. xvi. 19–20; xviii. 18; xix. 28; Luke xxii, 19, etc.). Their apostolic office, as would later become evident, was bound up with their having been not only chosen and instituted for it but companions of Christ throughout his mission as Messias, that is from the baptism of John to his ascension (Acts i. 21–22; cf. x. 37 and xiii. 31, read in conjunction with Mt. iii. 13; xvii. 55; Luke xxiii. 5). The apostolate is closely linked with Christ's life for us in the flesh—with his visible presence of those days, his powers and activities. It belongs to the sphere of the Incarnation, of the coming of the Son of Man, whose own mission it continues. Christ, in the discourse after the Last Supper, emphasises this important aspect, saying that he now sends his apostles as the Father had sent him (John xvii. 16 and 18), and that men will treat them as they treated him (John xiii. 20; xv. 18–21, 23; xvi. 2–3; xvii. 19; cf. Mt. x. 40; Luke x. 16; 1 John iv. 6 with John viii. 47). In fact, from the Father to him and from him to them, it is one and the same mission that flows and, in consequence, also the powers belonging to the mission (cf. John xvii. 18; 22–23; xx. 21)—the same mission which is, in the same degree, a mission of love.[1]

This is not the only case where we find two qualities, one of the purely spiritual or mystical sphere, the other a juridical one, conjoined in one and the same reality. The persistence of the mission which ensures the movement of *agape* on the part of God towards men is shown by the fact that the one sent and the person sending are equal in dignity, which is expressed in the Aramaic word for sent, *Saliah*. The one sent represents the person of his master and has the same authority; he is to be received in the same way as the master himself, from whom he has a power of attorney and whose functions he exercises in his absence. This is, undoubtedly, the whole idea of the apostolate instituted by Christ (cf. John xiii. 16, 20; xv. 20; xvii. 9 sq., especially 18; also Luke x. 16; Mt. x. 40).

The mission of the Holy Spirit is, in many ways, different from that of the apostles. It was not already inaugurated at the time of the Passion, but was then proclaimed as something in the future and made the subject of a promise (John xiv. 16, 26; xv. 26; xvi. 7–15; cf. vii. 39). It is not a consequence, like that of the apostles, of the Incarnation, the coming of the word in the flesh, which it was to continue, but is bound up with Christ's redemptive acts, with his passage to the Father and particularly with his glorification in heaven. It was necessary that Christ should go away, that he should be exalted, "glorified", for the Holy Spirit to be given (John vii. 39; xvi. 7, etc.). As regards Christ, the sending and the work of the Spirit are bound up with his condition of *Kyrios*, of domination over all things. The Holy Spirit indeed continues and accomplishes the work of Christ, but as linked with Christ's coming and his life in the flesh in a very different way from the apostles. The mission of the Holy Spirit is certainly presented as

[1] "As my Father sent me, so . . . ." corresponds exactly to "as the Father hath loved me, I also have loved you"—John, xv. 9; xvii. 23, 28.

a continuation of Christ's, but not precisely as *its* continuation. It is a distinct mission; he himself is another Paraclete[1], a Person distinct from Christ and one sent on a new mission which cannot be equated with that of the Incarnate word, though in close connection with it.

The relations between the two missions, close though they are, remain profoundly mysterious in spite of the abundance of texts from which we may derive some idea of them.

The mission or work of the Holy Spirit and the mission or work of Christ are homogeneous, in the first place, by reason of their purpose and content. From this point of view, the work of the Spirit is, indeed, the work of Christ. His function is to "bring to mind" all that Christ said (John xiv. 26; cf. xvi. 12 sq.), to bear witness to Christ (1 John iv. 1 sq.; John xv. 26; Apoc. xix. 10; cf. Acts i. 8). What he works in men has no other purpose or content than to bring to pass what Christ worked for the sake of men. This is one of the reasons why Scripture so often attributes spiritual activities indifferently to Christ (or the Lord) and to the Holy Spirit. It is unnecessary here to list all the places where the Christian is said to live, to sanctify himself, to feel peace and joy, to bear witness, etc., equally in and by the Holy Spirit and in and by Christ.[2] The identity of the work of each is such that it can be attributed indifferently to Christ and to the Spirit for, after all, the active presence of the latter is equivalent to that of Christ himself (John xiv. 18 sq.; xvi. 16, 22, 25). St. Paul himself says: "The Spirit we have been speaking of is the Lord" (2 Cor. iii. 17, and cf. 18). Our own conviction is, though we cannot argue it here, that this text can only be explained, that indeed the equivalence of action of Christ and the Spirit can only be explained ultimately by the profound Trinitarian concepts of the perfect

[1] ἄλλος (John xiv. 16). Christ had been a Paraclete to his followers, and he still is, in heaven (I John ii. 1).

[2] We find this even in the Gospels. Thus, the bearing of the disciples when brought to judgment is attributed to the Holy Spirit in Mt. x. 18–20 and Mark xiii. 10–12, and to Christ in St. Luke xxi. 12–15.

consubstantiality of the divine Persons, their circuminsession and perichoresis.

Though the Holy Spirit performs the very work of Christ, he has, none the less, his own special function whose nature is clearly indicated in the New Testament. Christ established an objective reality of grace and truth, of salvation and revelation; the Holy Spirit applies it to the interior of each of us. Christ effected once and for all, in himself, the union of mankind with God; the Spirit brings within its scope a vast number of individuals. Christ proclaimed the word of God; the Spirit brings it to the mind and inclines the heart to understand it. Christ built the house and the Spirit comes to dwell there (Eph. ii. 22). Christ gives us the quality of sons; the Spirit puts in our hearts the consciousness of this quality and makes us perform the corresponding acts and duties.[1] A more detailed study would reinforce and bring out fully these facts, which all lead up to the following conclusions—the mission of the Incarnate Word gives each individual soul, as it gave to the Church, existence in the new order of creation; it set up the structure of the Church and established an objective salvation with the various sources of grace and truth. The mission of the Holy Spirit makes these all produce their effects, gives the body of the Church its soul and brings the saving gifts to their fulfilment. Consequently, while acting always in accordance with the unique and decisive event of the Incarnation in time and "bringing to mind" what Christ said (John xiv. 26), the Holy Spirit continues to guide into all truth and to make plain what is still to come (John xvi. 13). He makes no innovations, he does not create anything that bears no relation to the work of Christ—this is a sufficient objection to the various movements based on an action of the Spirit independent of express relationship to the work

[1] Cf. Gal. iv. 4–6; Rom. viii. 15, and H. B. Swete, *The Holy Spirit in the New Testament*, London, 1909, pp. 204–206.

already accomplished by Christ.[1] What the Spirit does is to bring all to fulfilment. He takes, as it were beforehand, what is Christ's and makes it known to future ages (xvi. 15). He it is essentially who spoke by the prophets and brings into the Church a kind of prophetic dimension, a movement by which it is led to accomplish, right to the end, all that Christ placed in it in embryonic form. Between the two comings of Christ, between his departure and his return, the pasch he accomplished for us and that we shall celebrate with him, the Holy Spirit acts to bring all things to growth and fruitfulness.

The homogeneity of end and content between the work of Christ and that of the Spirit is due to a certain community of origin. This is not a community in every respect, a community of proximate principles, since the Holy Spirit is a Person distinct from the Word (incarnate), and each is the object of a special mission. It is true that all the divine actions *ad extra* are accomplished by the three Persons to whom the divine essence, wisdom and power, are strictly common. There is, however, in whatever slight degree, something "proper", without which the very words "mission" and "application" would have no real meaning. In the effects of grace, common indeed to all three Persons, there is something that corresponds mysteriously to what is proper to the Incarnate Word and the Holy Spirit, respectively.[2] Thus the distribution of properties between Christ's mission or work and the mission or work of the Spirit corresponds to something real; but by the very fact that the work or mission of each is distinct, those of the Spirit have a certain dependence on those of Christ.

[1] We refer in particular, as regards the past, to the ideas of Joachim de Flora on a Church of the Spirit following a Church of the Son, ideas which only escaped the censure they deserved because of Joachim's supporters in the Papal Curia. In our own time, certain interpretations of the spiritual technique of moral rearmament are open to the same kind of criticism.

[2] Even in the Latin and Thomist view (minimalist, in this context), it can be held that something is attributed to a divine Person, not as caused by him to the exclusion of the others, but as representing what is proper to that Person. Further, there is something impossible to specify exactly, yet real, a relation of each Person respectively to the essential attribute which represents them, namely, power, wisdom and love (or, as St. Paul says, love, grace, and communion—2 Cor. xiii, 13).

This is expressed in Scripture by the fact that the Spirit is sometimes said to be sent by the Father, but at the request and in the name of the Son (John xiv. 16, 26), and sometimes to be sent by Christ himself (John xv. 26; xvi. 7; Luke xxiv. 29; Acts ii. 23). Thus, in the order of the economy of grace, the procession or mission of the Spirit is dependent on the Word. It is a Catholic doctrine that this dependence in the sphere of the temporal "economy" supposes a dependence in that of existence in eternity; and this allows us to take in their fullest sense, not merely "economic" but ontological, the expressions used by St. Paul in speaking of the Spirit of Christ in the same sense in which he speaks elsewhere of the Spirit of God (Phil. i. 19; Gal. iv. 6; cf. with Rom. viii. 9 and 15; cf. 1 Peter i. 11; Acts xvi. 7).

It has often been observed that a theology which denies the eternal procession of the Holy Spirit from the Word tends to minimise the part played by definite forms or authority in actual life, and leaves the way more open to a kind of independent inspiration. The ecclesiology of the Orthodox Churches has a distinctly "pneumatic" tendency and declines to accept Catholic ideas of authority which seem to savour of legalism. This legalism, however, is closely bound up with values of profound mystical importance, as may be seen in the following passage from St. Thomas Aquinas which brings out strikingly the ecclesiological counterparts of the theology of the Holy Ghost: "To say that the Vicar of Christ, the Roman Pontiff, does not hold the Primacy in the universal Church is an error analogous to that which denies that the Holy Ghost proceeds from the Son. For Christ, the Son of God, consecrates his Church and consecrates it by the Holy Ghost as by his seal or stamp. Likewise, the Vicar of Christ by his primacy and governance, like a good servant, preserves the universal Church that is subject to Christ . . .".[1] In fact, one cannot

[1] *Contra errores Graecorum*, lio. 2, prol.: "In our own day, too, there are those who dissolve Christ and do their utmost to lessen his dignity. They do so when they say that the Holy Ghost does not proceed from the Son, whereas the latter is his *Spirator* together with the Father. Along with this, when they deny that there is a head of the Church, the holy Roman Church, they clearly dissolve the unity of the mystical body, for they cannot be a single body if there is not a single head, any more than a community without a ruler."

fail to notice the way in which Christ speaks of his Church (Mt. xvi. 18), his sheep (John x. 1–16; xxi. 15–17), and how St. Paul speaks of Christ as "head of the Church, his body, of which he is the Saviour, having given himself up on its behalf . . . to summon it into his own presence . . ." (Eph. v. 23, 25, 26; cf. Acts xx. 28). Now Christ, as we know, builds up his Church by means of *his* apostles and *his* Spirit. These might almost be called his agents whom he has empowered to execute his work in the time of his absence, his "vicars", in fact; so, at any rate, his apostles are called in the liturgy (*quos operis tui vicarios*—Preface of the Apostles). Later, we will consider how the same expression may be used of the Holy Spirit. At the moment, we must examine more closely the relationship of these two agents to the Incarnation itself and its end.

This relationship may be expressed in two propositions: (1) what brings to pass the work of Christ proceeds from Christ himself in his Incarnation and (2) connects the seed with its fruit, the source to its fullness, the Alpha that is Christ acting alone for our sakes to the Omega which we are to be with and in him, from him and for him. Thus, the agents of Christ's work have a backward-looking relationship (if we may so express it) to his incarnation in time and a forward-looking one to its consummation at the end of the world. They function, in fact, throughout the whole of the interval between the two comings of Christ and this is, precisely, the time of the Church.

It has already been pointed out that the Church as an institution, which precedes and builds up the Church as a community of believers, consists of the deposit of faith, the deposit of the sacraments of faith and that of the apostolic powers bringing both faith and sacraments to men. It is from these that the Church derives its structure. Now it is essential to realize that they all come directly from what Christ was and did for us in the time of his earthly life. This is clear enough as regards the deposit of faith. Provided we do not exclude the revelation given by the prophets and the apostles, whose essential message is concerned with Christ, we may say that Christ himself is the revelation, the word of God, and he makes known to us the supreme mystery of the Father, the Son and the Spirit. As to the sacraments, they all derive from Christ's institution. This is brought out by St. John, both symbolically and literally, in regard to baptism and the Eucharist, the two greater sacraments and the most necessary to salvation, those Christ himself conferred and whose matter he directly determined and sanctified. St. John, in the epistle perhaps intended as an introduction to his gospel, tells us that Christ came by water and blood (1 John v. 6), and shows us, in a passage of exceptional solemnity, this water and blood flowing from the side of Christ as he hung on the cross, dead but still warm (John xix. 34 sq.). According to the commentators, he intended, in accord with the whole tone of his gospel and the content of his witness, to show thereby the intimate connection of Christ's mystical presence with his historical reality, the relation of the Christ of faith with the Christ who lives interiorly in his followers, with the Christ who came in the flesh.[1] This teaching is confined to St. John. According to St. Paul as well, the sacraments link the Church and the whole Christian life to the historical Christ who instituted them, and to his death. As with the apostolate (see above), all that exercises a kind of vicarious presence and action of Christ is expressly bound up with his *acta et passa in carne*.

It is significant that, in neglecting to take proper account of these solid scriptural data, those who, for reasons of system, minimize the institutional aspect of the Church and see it only as the community of believers, see it too in connection with Pentecost, with the risen Christ, rather than with the "Christ of history" and with his *acta et passa in carne*.

Yet the actual sending of the Holy Spirit is strongly and explicitly connected by St. John to the coming and passion of Christ, just as are the elements of the Church's institution. Like

[1] For the sacramental interpretation of the blood and water, see E. C. Hoskyns, *The Fourth Gospel*, 2nd ed., 1947, pp. 552 sqq.

the sacraments, too, the fact is expressed in various places sometimes in symbolical form, sometimes literally. It is stated clearly in the celebrated passage of John vii. 39, whose interpretation, about which all are agreed, is basically independent of the punctuation or meaning of the two preceding verses: "The Spirit had not yet been given to men, because Jesus had not yet been raised to glory". To this statement corresponds the symbol of Calvary, whether, on the basis of John vii. 39, we see, in the water flowing from the side of Christ, the Holy Spirit, bound up with the blood of Christ's glorification, or else, seeing in the blood and water the sacraments, we consider the Spirit referred to in John xix, 36: "Then he bowed his head and yielded up his spirit".[1] In both cases, the sending of the Spirit is connected with the Passion, with the immolated body of the incarnate Word, the Lamb that the Apocalypse shows us sitting with God on a single throne whence flows the river of eternal life (Apoc. xxii, 1 sq.). Yet another passage of St. John shows clearly the connection of the Spirit of Pentecost with the acts and the mystery of Christ. On the very evening of the Pasch, the risen Christ came into the midst of his disciples, breathed on them and said: "Receive ye the Holy Spirit. . . ." The word used here, it has been pointed out, is expressive of the way in which a creation or a re-creation, a healing or destruction is wrought.[2] The new creation of Pentecost is directly linked up by St. John to Christ. Some writers are even of the opinion that John, to emphasise this connection, intended to place Pentecost, in a way, on the very day of the Pasch, not, of course, in a historical sense, as actually occurring then, but symbolically and doctrinally, as indicating the significance of the facts. As to the historical Pentecost, the word itself is sufficient indica-

1 Thus Hoskyns, *The Fourth Gospel*, 2nd ed., London, 1947, pp. 530, 532; L. S. Thornton in *The Apostolic Ministry*, London, 1946, pp. 98, sq. 9, and an allusion in *The Common Life in the Body of Christ*, (2nd ed. 1944, p. 416). The same idea is taken up by Mascall, *Christ, the Christian and the Church*, London, 1946, p. 133.

2 Hoskyns, "Genesis i—iii and St. John's Gospel," in *Journal of Theological Studies* 21 (1920), pp. 210–218, cf. p. 215; *The Fourth Gospel*, p. 547.

tion of what it was, namely, the fiftieth day of the Paschal feast, the fullness and the fruit of the Pasch of the Lord. Liturgists are constantly pointing out that Pentecost is a part of the Christological cycle, that it completes the cycle of the Pascal economy, forming, as it does, with the Pasch one single feast. From then on, Christ's work is not carried out for us in his own Person exclusively, but is spread throughout his whole body, until the fullness of time comes which will bring in the Pasch of the parousia.

Can we call the Holy Spirit the "vicar" of Christ, as we have seen the liturgy calls the apostles? Tertullian has no hesitation in so doing; but, despite his admitted genius in the use of language and the great influence he exercised on the development of the theological vocabulary of the western Church, he has not been followed in this. The traditional use prefers vaguer expressions, which convey the idea that the Holy Spirit does the work of Christ[1], but without suggesting that he acts only through the power of Christ, as is the case with the apostles. Tertullian was basically concerned with expressing, in a somewhat rigid legal terminology, the great design of the Father sending the Son who, jointly with the Father, sends the Holy Spirit. The Fathers were fond of stressing this descending order, followed by a reverse order of ascent by which the Holy Spirit effects the work of Christ who, in turn, when all has been subjected to him, will give homage to him who has subjected all things to him (1 Cor. xv. 28). In this sense, there is indeed a kind of vicarious action of the Holy Spirit in relation to Christ and of Christ in relation to the Father, the one acting as if on account of the other. The Spirit, since he acts in conjunction with the Church in the interval between Christ's departure and return, desires, too, along with the Church, this return (Apoc. xxii. 17). Swete observes that, after his return, Christ will himself exercise this function of guiding the faithful, for which, at the time of his departure, he had

[1] The encyclical *Mystici Corporis,* 1943, says: "The divine Redeemer sent the Spirit of truth, who, performing his own function . . . ."

promised he would send the Spirit.[1] This might lead us to think that the action of the Spirit has a mediatory quality corresponding to a vicarious function, in some such way as Christ's action until the time when he shall have handed all things over to the Father so that God may be all in all. Yet neither Christ in relation to the Father, nor the Spirit in relation to Christ, is in the same position as the apostles. These, indeed, were set up, in every respect, by the mandate given to them and, once they have discharged it, they will have nothing more to do as regards our access to God. The Holy Spirit and Christ, on the other hand, always retain their role in our regard. In heaven, Christ remains our high priest for ever. The Holy Spirit is always the living water (Apoc. vii. 16 sq.; xxii. 1 sq.; cf. John iv. 14); he is not merely a vicar, he does not simply exercise a "ministry" of the Incarnate Word, he is not an "instrument". For all these reasons, even if we confine ourselves to our present subject, that of the agency of Christ's work, his position is very different from that of the apostles.

None the less, he works along with them, in the period between the two comings of Christ; they, in fact, are sent as the specific realizors of his work in that interval. To this is due the fact that, in the function each discharges, there is one aspect turned, as it were, towards the past, to the historical facts of the incarnation and Pasch of Christ, from which all has its origin, and another aspect turned toward the future, to the fulfilment of the mystery of Christ throughout the range of his entire Mystical Body. In this connection, we may here, as we have done earlier, add to the apostles the other elements of the institutional Church, namely the deposit of faith and of the sacraments of faith. The entire ecclesiastical or apostolic institution it is, on the one hand, and the Holy Spirit, on the other, which, at the same time, bear reference to the Incarnation, whence they come, and to the final fulfilment.

The first aspect of their mission is that it assures homogeneity from Alpha to Omega; the homogeneity, that is, of all that is to

[1] Apoc. vii. 17; John xvi. 13—the same word in each case. Cf. Swete, *op. sit.*, p. 357.

develop in that period and of all that will be garnered at its term with what was laid down in the beginning. Each assures this in his own province, the apostolate and the institutional Church in that of the external means of grace and their objective identity with those which Christ set up in the exercise of his messianic power as king, prophet and priest. The real meaning of the apostolate and the hierarchy is, as we have shown elsewhere, that they ensure, in the visible order in which we live and where the Body of Christ is to be realized, that all comes from the one single event of the Incarnation and Pasch of Christ. But what the apostolic body and the institutional Church effect in the exterior and objective order the Holy Spirit does within the institution itself and within individuals. He speaks and bears witness, but he does not speak of himself; he says what he has heard; he receives of Christ to declare it to us (John xvi. 13–15).[1] He brings each one into possession of the gift of Christ, and so brings about between all of them and Christ that identity we call mystical for want of any adequate analogy in the natural order. In this way, there comes into being that single reality which is both Church and Body of Christ, built up by what has its origin in him, Head and Principle, Alpha and First-born of all.

Thus the Holy Spirit and the Apostolate receive from what pertains to Christ only in order to procure for him the building-up of his body, the maturity of completed growth (Eph. iv. 12–13). Christ is, at once, the Alpha and the Omega (Apoc. i. 8; xxi. 6; xxii. 13), and this well expresses the unity of the term with the beginning. But he is Alpha himself alone, although he is so for our sakes, whereas he is Omega together with us or we are so together with him, as forming a single body with him who is its origin. In absolute strictness, there is only one who goes up to heaven, he who came down from heaven (John iii. 13); but we

[1] This is shown in the letters to the seven Churches of the Apocalypse. They are called upon to hear "what the Spirit says to the Churches" (II, 7, 11, 17, 29; III, 6, 13, 22), yet, at the beginning of each message, it is Christ who is said to be speaking (II, 1, 8, 12, 18; III, 1, 7, 14).

ascend in him. It is the same mystery, the same Pasch, but, between its first and its final moment, in that interval between the ascension and the parousia, which is the time of the Church, there is communication and growth. The same passages which say that the Spirit will proclaim what he has heard point to him as leading the disciples into all truth, teaching them all things, making known what is to come (John xiv. 16; xiv. 13); the apostles are to do, in a sense, greater things than Christ (xiv. 12); through them, through us, all things are to grow up into him who is the head, the Christ (Eph. iv. 15), so that he may be "fulfilled" in all (i. 23).

It is this double law of identity and development, of reference to the unique fact of the historical incarnation, revelation, pasch and apostolate and, at the same time, a law of presence, of activity and growth throughout space and time, which is the law of the Church, placed as it is between the pasch and the parousia to be the living link between them. Under the direction of the great principles of identity of which we have spoken, the *agi* of men is joined to the *datum* of God, in such wise that this latter is lived by all those to whom it has been predestined. The "passage" of Christ is celebrated, in baptism, the Eucharist and the other sacraments, after the manner which is characteristic of the liturgy, referring both to the past event, of which the sacrament is the memorial, and to the final fulfilment; in this way what Christ did flows into and fills the whole of time, which is made use of to prepare the plenitude of the parousia. Here we have to do with the whole Christian meaning of time, the entire significance of the time of the Church. This significance is to be found in that *agi* of the *datum* through which, between the Alpha and the Omega, a function is enacted in no merely mechanical way, a function of such a sort that, at its term, there is found once again the same single reality set up at the beginning, like the talent shamefacedly buried, of which the Gospel speaks.

This law is seen at work, not only in the case of the sacraments in their relation to the messianic acts and the passion accomplished once and for all, but also as regards Tradition in its relation to

Scripture, development in relation to Revelation and the apostolate in relation to the mission of Christ. In each of these, in its own specific way, there is a single *datum*, an *agi* of this *datum* in time and space, a kind of "recommencement", as Péguy calls it, a development and growth towards a fulfilment which yet will be found to contain nothing which is not derived from the initial stage.

(2) *The Holy Spirit and the apostolic institution act jointly to bring about the Body of Christ*

This joint action is to be seen, both in the ministry in general, its constitution, authority and effects and, more particularly, in its two principal functions, those connected with the word and the sacraments.

The apostles are such "by the Holy Spirit" (Acts i. 2; xiii. 4). The Holy Spirit and the apostles are manifested jointly at Pentecost; not that the apostolate had not been founded beforehand or that the Spirit had not already been given, but it was at Pentecost that the Church was definitely set up in the world and manifested as a new creation with its own specific energies, which consist precisely in the Holy Spirit and the apostolic ministry acting conjointly (cf. John xx. 22–23).

From Pentecost onwards, the apostolate and the Spirit act in conjunction and the expansion of the Church is continuously brought about by their action; the witnesses to the Gospel are filled with the Holy Spirit (Acts iv. 8; xiii. 9; ii. 4, etc.), and are guided by him even in the details of their activities (x. 19; viii. 29, 39, etc.). As has often been remarked, the whole of the Acts could very well be summarized in the verse: "The Church . . . became firmly established, guided by the fear of God, and grew in numbers by the help of the Holy Spirit" (ix. 31); we might equally well translate, "by the invocation of the Holy Spirit".

The Spirit does not only join in with the ministry in its work, but intervenes to establish and consecrate it, or rather to bring about interiorly and in reality the consecration imparted in a visible manner by ministers already instituted; thus the prophets and doctors of Antioch lay hands on Saul and Barnabas, but the latter are also said to be sent by the Holy Spirit (Acts xiii. 3 and 4); likewise, St. Paul appoints the elders by imposition of hands (xiv. 22), but, in addressing those of Ephesus, he says: "Keep watch, then, over yourselves, and over God's Church, in which the Holy Spirit has made you bishops" (xx. 28). The consecration of ministers is jointly the work of the Holy Spirit and the apostolic body. The authority of the apostles is, as it were, equated with that of God himself. Thus, Ananias, in attempting to deceive the apostles, in reality lied to the Holy Spirit and to God (v. 3 and 4); and later, at the synod of Jerusalem, the apostles and elders made use in an official statement, legal in tone, of the celebrated formula: "It has seemed good to the Holy Ghost and to us" (xv. 28). It is a formula that recalls those of the councils of the Greek or Jewish world, in which is expressed a decision, not of an individual acting on his own judgment, but of a group of persons in communion with one another. Here there is a sort of sanhedrin of the Church, consisting of the apostles and elders, but their decision is taken in communion with the Holy Spirit himself, the chief personage, if we may dare to say so, of the council, whose authority is applied in conjunction with that of the apostles and elders.

The ultimate end and outcome of a ministry associated in this way with the Holy Spirit in its very constitution, in its authority and its acts, is the building up of the body of Christ. The apostolic ministry issues in the gift of the Holy Spirit (Acts viii. 14–17; x. 44; xix. 6). So it is not surprising to see St. Paul looking on the community of Corinth, formed by him, as a letter from Christ, written by him, not with ink, but with the Spirit of the living God (2 Cor. iii. 2–3); he is speaking of a spiritual gift, but of a gift which is always bound up with the Person of the Holy Spirit. From the same point of view, it is very significant that, in the great texts where St. Paul speaks of the unity and life of the body, he brings into relation the unity of the spirit on the one hand, and the multiplicity of members on the other (1 Cor. xii. 12 sq.; Eph. iv. 4 sq.).

There is, too, the same association and co-operation of the Spirit with the two great acts of the ministry, the preaching of the word and the celebration of the sacraments.

In the first place, since the apostles were made such by the Holy Spirit, they were also made by him men of the word. They receive him and, immediately, they speak (Acts ii. 4; iv. 31, 33). It is by the Holy Spirit sent from heaven that the ministers of the Gospel proclaim and preach (1 Peter i. 12). Once more, Christ's work is taken up after his departure by his two envoys, the Holy Spirit and the apostolic body. Christ taught (Mt. v. 2; vii. 29; Jn. vi. 59), but he arranged for the apostles to continue teaching after him (Mt. xxviii. 20; cf. v. 19), and for the Holy Spirit as well (Jn. xiv. 26; cf. Lk. xii. 12). He even proclaimed expressly the law governing the joint action and agreement concerning the testimony given at one and the same time by the Holy Spirit and the apostles—"when the Spirit . . . whom I will send to you from the Father's side, he will bear witness of what I was; and you too are to be my witnesses, you who from the first have been in my company" (Jn. xv. 26–27). Thus when Christ appoints the apostles his witnesses, he links up their testimony to the sending of the Spirit (Lk. xxiv. 48–49; Acts i. 8).

On the joint witness of the apostles and the Holy Spirit there exist many excellent studies, but no complete treatise. The apostles are not witnesses in a merely historical aspect, with a view to securing a purely objective recording and acknowledgment of the facts. They are witnesses solely as ministers of the Gospel, in their function of proclaiming the good news of salvation in Christ. Consequently their testimony is, in part, a narrative of the events in the life of Christ all the time they were with him, what they themselves had seen and heard and also, as was Christ's own preaching, an appeal to the prophecies and the fulfilment of all that was declared about Christ and of the preparations for his coming in the Old Testament. But it is, in addition, as Asting rightly points out, a proclamation of the future accomplishment of the messianic acts; for, as we have seen, the apostolate and the Church as constituted by Christ, along with the Holy Spirit, are constantly at work in the interval between Christ's pasch and parousia to link up and urge on the Alpha of the former to the Omega of the latter. In the testimony of the apostles, the connection between the facts as already having occurred and their fulfilment in the body of Christ is brought out clearly in many places, particularly in 1 Jn. i. 1–3 and Acts v. 30–32—"It was the God of our fathers that raised up Jesus, the man you hung on a gibbet to die. It is God who raised him up to his own right hand, as the prince and Saviour who is to bring Israel repentance and remission of sins. Of this we are witnesses; we and the Holy Spirit God gives to all those who obey him".

How does the Holy Spirit give this testimony? First, he gave it, and continues to give it, in the prophets—(cf. Heb. x. 15; iii. 7; ix. 8; Acts x. 43, etc.). He does so by the strength he imparts to the apostles in their witnessing—"They were all filled with the Holy Spirit, and began to preach the word of God with confidence.... Great was the power with which the apostles testified to the resurrection of our Lord Jesus Christ, and great was the grace that rested on them all" (Acts iv. 31–33). In the great judicial process going on after Christ's departure, a kind of revision or, at any rate, a continuation of what he endured, which will last as long as there is a "world", while the apostles bear witness "unto the ends of the earth", the Holy Spirit will "convince the world of sin" (Jn. xvi. 8); whether it is that he brings the world to awareness of its sin, or that he strengthens in the apostles their conviction that the world is wrong and that Christ's cause is just, in short, that he refutes the world and brings out clearly its sin to the consciousness of the faithful, according to an interpretation not, indeed, widely accepted but well-founded. At all events, one essential aspect of the testimony of the Holy Spirit is to manifest the sin of the world and to strengthen the faithful interiorly. We know too that he does not leave the ministers of the Gospel to themselves, but acts as their guide (cf. above and Acts xx. 22–23). God accompanies them too, "bearing them witness by signs and wonders and divers miracles and distributions of the Holy Ghost according to his will" (Heb. ii. 3–4: God himself "witnesses with"; cf. 1 Thess. i. 5).

In addition to the testimony the Holy Ghost gives by external signs and within the apostles themselves there is that which he gives within those who hear them. In a general way, he brings about within souls a work corresponding to that effected by the apostolate externally, the work of conversion and salvation by the preaching and reception of the Gospel. His work begins with a *call*. It has been justly emphasized that the act of calling or vocation is prominent among all the divine acts which result in the "convocation", that is in the Church. Without unduly stressing the associated meanings of Κλῆσις, Καλεῖν, 'Εκκαλεῖν, 'Εκκλησῖα, we must observe the relation between the call and the setting up of the Church; the people of God is gathered and constituted from the time of its being called, of its Κλησις. This is an act of God, proceeding from his free and eternal plan, an act most intimate and secret (Rom. viii. 28, 30, etc.); but this call of God is shown forth outwardly and concretely by the apostolic preaching of the Gospel (2 Thess. ii. 13, with which cf. Rom. x. 14 sq.), and this preaching is itself accompanied by an act of the Holy Spirit which is a kind of urgent call and prompting, the "paraclesis" by which, we are told in the Acts (ix. 31), the Church is built up and develops. Thus, vocation, the divine act which, in God, follows upon election, is manifested to men by a twofold call to faith, one exterior, by the apostolic word, the other interior, by the prompting, the invitation and the drawing of which the Holy Spirit is the originator (cf. St. Thomas, *In Rom.*, c. 8, lec. 6). To this corresponds the inclination of the heart, its readiness to answer the call and receive the word, of which the book of the Acts (xvi. 14, 1: Lydia) speaks, and after it, the whole Christian tradition (cf. ix. 6; x. 5; *Summa Theol.*, II^{a}–II^{ae}, q. 177, a. I). In this way, the Holy Spirit begins the movement of conversion which he continues by stirring up in us a conviction of sin, a rooted feeling of the need to change our life and to be truly converted. The Holy Spirit, too, makes us hear in the heart, as if directly and actually spoken to us, the calls of the scriptural witness: "If you hear his voice speaking to you this day, do not harden your hearts . . . (Heb. iii. 7). If this witness, and that of the preacher of the Gospel, is received, the Holy Spirit gives us the grace of faith itself, for "it is only through the Holy Spirit that anyone can say, Jesus is the Lord" (1 Cor. xii. 3). He pursues his work further in the whole *vita in Christo,* which is life on the basis of faith, by testifying to our spirit that, being forgiven, we are sons of God (Rom. viii. 16; 1 Jn. iii. 19–24), by praying in us (Rom. viii. 26–27), instructing us in all things by his presence and the interior certainty he brings, by penetrating us deeply with his unction (Jn. xvi. 13; 1 Jn. ii. 20–27).

The New Testament does not speak so expressly about the life and sacramental practise of the faithful as it does about the preaching of the apostles, but all the positive data it contains have been faithfully followed out and developed in liturgical and theological tradition.

The connection of the Spirit with Baptism and his working in it are quite evident, both from the proclamation of the baptism of the Spirit to be given by Christ (Mt. iii. 1; Mark i. 8; Luke iii. 16) and from Christ's own baptism, in which, to signify the institution of the baptism of the Spirit, the dove rested upon Christ (John i. 32-33; cf. Mark i. 10), as well as from Christ's discourse to Nicodemus on the new birth from water and the Spirit (John iii. 5) and the actual teaching and practice of the apostles (Acts xix. 2–6; 1 Cor. xii. 13, etc.). We find, too, a similar connection of the Spirit with the sacrament of Penance (John x. 23), with the imposition of hands to impart the fullness of spiritual gifts (Acts viii. 14–17, 18; ix. 17; xix. 6), with the imposition of hands for the exercise of the ministry (Acts xiii. 2–4; cf. 1 Tim. iv. 14 and 2 Tim. i. 6)—even, in some respects, with the Eucharist, so closely bound up with the work of the

Spirit,[1] and with the anointing of the sick, which is accompanied with prayer and invocation of the name of the Lord, that is to say with an "epiclesis" (James v. 14).

Each of these topics calls for a special study, but here we are only concerned with the function of the Holy Spirit in the working of the sacraments and his connection with the visible actions performed by the Christian ministry. Theologically speaking, we have here one of the foundations of the necessity for an intervention of the Holy Spirit in the sacraments and, therefore, for an epiclesis. The question of the epiclesis, which has, anyhow, been somewhat artificially restricted to the eucharistic epiclesis, has been obscured by the secondary problem of the precise moment of the consecration; and has been even more fundamentally impaired through being treated in the theology of the sacraments, whereas it can be properly understood only as part of the theology of the Holy Spirit. We hope to return to this one day, as we cannot delay on it here; it is enough to point out its connection with our present subject, which derives from the fact that the Holy Spirit is, jointly with the apostolic ministry or the institutional Church, the active principle realizing the work of Christ. Their common function is that of applying throughout space and time the universal cause of salvation, of life reconciled in and through Christ. The specific function of the Holy Spirit is, on the one hand, to give the institution life and movement (and, in this sense of the word, efficacity) and, on the other hand, to bring to individuals and to their innermost being the gifts of God.

If we look for the principle of this joint working of the Holy Spirit with the apostolic ministry or the institutional Church, we come to his function in the actual constitution of the universal cause of salvation, namely Christ himself. The very first coming of the Spirit, his first union with a human agency which was to

[1] Cf. John vi. 62–63 (everything to do with "spirit" involves the action of the "Spirit"); according to St. Paul, the eucharist and the Spirit both produce the same effect, namely, the unity of a single body (I Cor. v. 17 and xii. 13; Eph. lv. 4).

co-operate with him, resulted in the conception of Christ "incarnated of the Holy Spirit and the Virgin Mary", in the words of the creed of Nicea and Constantinople. That was, indeed, the first and decisive coming of Christ among us, but his real "entry" as the Messias came with his baptism by John (Εἰσῆλθεν—Acts i. 21). Christ himself, as well as his disciples, called his baptism the beginning (John xv. 27; Luke i. 2; iii. 23; cf. Acts x. 37). John was, indeed, the precursor and even the consecrator of Christ; his function has been appropriately compared to that of Samuel in regard to David, the type of the Messias-King. Now, as the Spirit came down on Mary for the conception of Christ, he came down on Christ at his baptism to consecrate him for the messianic ministry. As he did formerly on David, the type of the Messias-King (1 Kings xvi. 3), on the royal branch foretold as issuing from him (Isaias xi. 1–2), on the Servant prophetically described by Isaias (xiii. 1; lxi. 1–3; cf. Luke iv. 17–21), the Spirit came down on Jesus and rested on him. That here we have the origin and the reason of the joint action of the Spirit and the water of Baptism is obvious enough, but it means something more. The consecration by the Spirit at Christ's baptism was his consecration to the messianic ministry. He had been sanctified in himself from his conception (Luke i. 35), and now he was sanctified in view of the ministry, and so as source of grace for us, at his baptism as Messias. For this reason, he is, a second time, called Son—and would be, a third time, in the mystery of his "passage", his death-resurrection-ascension (Acts xiii. 33)—as if sent into the world a second time, as source of grace, in whom the Father was well pleased (Luke iii. 22). At his incarnation, the Word of God espoused our human nature as to its being and life, so as to share our human manner of life; at his baptism, he espoused the Church—and this espousal was to be consummated in the mystery of his pasch, by which the sacraments and the whole work of the ministry would become efficacious. He espoused, not human nature as such, but the Church, the organism of the messianic work, the visible body containing the means of grace and constituted such from the moment of his baptism. Christ was constituted Son of God at his conception, but was declared Son and became such *for us* at his baptism, in which was instituted the baptism of the Spirit, that of our own sonship. This was the beginning of the sacramental order, of the order of the ministry and of that association of the Spirit with each which has been the theme of the preceding pages. The foundation of the union between the Holy Spirit and the institutional Church is the union of operation present, from the beginning, between the Holy Spirit and Christ. This union, deriving from the mystery of the divine being, of the eternal relations in God, of the consubstantiality and circuminsession of the divine Persons, was proclaimed, as regards Christ, at his baptism and, as regards the Church and the apostolate, at Pentecost, their baptism by the Holy Spirit.

We are now in a position to state more precisely the nature of the union of the Holy Spirit with the institutional Church founded by Christ in his life on earth. The union is not incarnational, despite the analogies various distinguished writers have pointed out[1]; consequently, however mysterious and difficult to formulate are the relations between the Spirit and Christ, the Spirit and the Mystical Body, the latter is not the body of the Holy Spirit but of Christ. Not only is the action of the Holy Spirit wholly relative to Christ and is to effect within the disciples, after Christ's departure, the same as he did while still with them[2], but the Spirit came to give life, motion and effectiveness to a body, to sacraments, to an apostolic ministry already constituted and constituted by Christ, in the time of his *acta et passa in carne*. It has been repeatedly shown by Catholic writers

[1] Analogies between the Spirit's coming at baptism and his coming at the Annunciation (Swete, *The Holy Spirit in the N.T.*, p. 46), between the bond that Jn. iii. 4 points to between the Spirit and the water and that existing the Word and the flesh. Manning proposed, at the Vatican Council, that the bond between the Holy Spirit and the Church should be conceived "juxta incarnationis analogiam, seclusa tamen unione hypostatica".

[2] Christ was with his own (Jn. xv. 5), who were to remain in him, with him, and keep his word; they would do this by the Holy Spirit (xiv. 25 sq.; xvi. 22 sq.).

that Christ instituted a ministry, a body of doctrine, sacraments, a Church, before his pasch, though the sacraments received their efficacity from his Passion, and the hierarchical mission of the apostles was definitely given only after the resurrection. Many non-Catholic writers express themselves on this subject in just the same way as we would.[1] In this connection, it would doubtless be appropriate to make use of the categories of *structure* and *life* we have already suggested earlier. No doubt, too, there could be found, in the various parts of the Bible which speak of a creation, significant analogies suggesting a kind of law of God's working—the creation of Adam (Gen. ii. 7), the vision of Ezechiel (xxxviii)—a function of the Spirit of completing a work already laid out in its structure or skeleton. First comes the organization, and afterwards life and movement; first the letter, afterwards the understanding.[2] Accordingly, the Holy Ghost comes essentially for the purpose of animating and giving movement to a body constituted by Christ and which is his body; he is, for the threefold deposit of the faith, the sacraments and the apostolic powers, what the vital principle is for an organism.

We can understand that Tradition gives the Holy Ghost the title of soul of the Church. It is not, however, to be taken in the sense of a soul entering into composition with the body of the Church and being united to it in a physical and substantial union, like our souls and bodies. There is no question of an incarnation, of union in actual being, such that all the actions of the Church would be physically and personally the actions of the Holy Ghost and have no other subject of attribution than him. They certainly come from him, but also from that body instituted by Christ as a subject in its own right, a collective person, which he himself called "my Church", the Church we know too to be

1 This is quite usual in Anglican writers, whose ecclesiology is closely linked with the Incarnation. See, in particular, Wotherspoon, *The Ministry in the Church in relation to Prophecy and Spiritual Gifts* (*charismata*), London, 1916, pp. 103 sqq.

2 Christ taught; his dsciples were to understand later. There is a whole theology of the apostolic witness and of the relations between Scripture and Tradition to be developed in this connection.

his spouse. This is not the place to try and work out what is the inmost reality of this body or quasi-person which is the Church. For our present purpose, it is sufficient to point out that the Holy Spirit does not enter into composition with it as a form with matter, but united himself with it as with a subject already constituted in being. So it is that Scripture makes use of expressions which suggest the idea, not of a soul as a part of a composite being, but of one indwelling and acting: *to be with* always (John xvi. 16), *to be given* (ibid.), *to be present*, *to inhabit*, as if in a sanctuary, to be given by God as something one has (1 Cor. iii. 16; vi. 19), and of which one can be filled. In addition, there are all the texts, of which we have already cited a fair number and which may be found in a concordance, where all kinds of operations are attributed to the Holy Spirit—bearing witness, causing a rebirth, praying, guiding, teaching, etc. It is clear that, if these operations imply what we may call an ontic ontology or physical production, the texts which express the relation of the Holy Spirit to the Church in terms of *habitation*, *being with*, imply an intersubjective ontology. The Holy Spirit does not inform the Church by entering into a physical composition with it to constitute a single substantial being which is both divine and human; he is with it to guide and assist it, to enable it to perform actions which, while outwardly human, are bearers of a divine virtue, *virtus Spiritus Sancti*.

What sort of a union, then, is it, if it is not one of actual being? It is a union of alliance, grounded on God's decree for man's salvation and on his promises, that is to say on the design of grace God is to realize in the time fixed by him. Since the good envisaged rests on a decree and promise of God, it has the strongest and most certain warrant conceivable, infinitely more solid and assured than any bond created by an undertaking and a promise on the part of man. Now, if God pledged himself, under the old disposition of his alliance, to succour his people, guide and strengthen them, he has pledged himself, under the regime of the new and final disposition made in the blood of Jesus, to give his Spirit in such a way that it really dwells in the new Israel. The Spirit is the specific gift of the messianic era. He rested on Christ in all his fullness; but this fullness Christ, raised up to heaven, communicated to his own (Jn. i. 16; Acts ii. 33). The Spirit, after having come at Pentecost in fulfilment of the promise of the Father and of Christ (Lk. xxiv. 49; Jn. xiv. 16, etc.), remains with the Church and the "acts of the apostles" that St. Luke relates were to such a degree guided and accomplished by the Spirit that the *Acts* have been called the Gospel of the Holy Spirit. The regime of the new and final disposition is a regime of an abiding gift, of a permanent presence and assistance, closely bound up with a *being with* which is an indwelling. The post-pentecostal ministry is a "ministry of the Spirit" (2 Cor. ii. 4–18).

If the Holy Spirit is the soul of Christ's Mystical Body, and if he is, as we have shown, conjoined with the institutional Church and the apostolic body—these latter doing externally and visibly what he himself does interiorly—it might be said that the elements of the institutional Church and the apostolic body are, externally, the soul of the Church as the Holy Spirit is its soul internally. This, indeed, is held by some of the Fathers, and the same idea is developed by Journet in *The Church of the Word Incarnate*. However, in view both of tradition and of speculative theology, we prefer to reserve the title of soul of the Church to the Holy Spirit exclusively and to speak of formal cause or formal principles in connection with the exterior elements of the institution or of the apostolic powers.

Whatever be the terms employed, it remains that the certainty of God's promise and the union of alliance existing between the Church and the Holy Spirit are the ground of the infallibility of the hierarchical actions, of those, that is, by which the visible Church receives visibly its structure and is linked, by the visible bond of apostolicity, to Christ's institution. The relevant passages of the New Testament are well known and, in any case, fully developed in Catholic works on the subject of the Church. The Acts, too, and the Epistles obviously suppose that the apostolic ministry performs the actual work of God and by the power of God. But from these texts to those of the apostolic Fathers, Clement and Ignatius; from the latter to St. Irenaeus, St. Cyprian and the Fathers of the classical era; from these to the affirmations of the Councils claiming their own decisions to be those of the Holy Spirit himself, as the synod of Jerusalem had done before; finally, from all this to the statements of classical theology, of the Magisterium, even to those of the most exact scholastic theory speaking of immediacy of *virtus* in the *mediatio suppositi,* where can be found any breach in the consciousness and the vindication of the fact that, thanks to the bond of alliance between the Holy Spirit and the institutional Church, the latter, in those major actions concerning its very structure, enjoys the guarantee of God's promises and, for that reason, of some kind of infallibility?

Why, indeed, should it not? In the natural order, for example, we see God intervening, so to speak, to give an immortal soul to what the union of man and woman has placed in an existence which was, in the first instance, an animal one. God, as St. Thomas shows, must give directly, and alone can give, the first and the final spiritual perfection, the immortal soul and deifying grace. He gives the soul by his unfailing co-operation with the human work of the flesh, faithfully observing the laws of his own creation; why, then, should he not give his grace in co-operation with the visible work of the apostolic ministry, faithful in this to the institution of the alliance sealed in the blood of Christ? On these lines we come, not merely to a reconciliation—which is absolutely demanded by Catholic tradition—but to a perfect equation of the *Ecclesia-numerus Episcoporum* and the *Ecclesia-Spiritus* which Tertullian, as a Montanist, tried to separate and oppose.

None the less, in the spiritual sphere and, particularly, in that of grace, a kind of physical sequence of cause and effect is not the whole of what theology has to say. All that we have said so far is true enough: there is a union of alliance, grounded in the will of God, between the Holy Spirit and the institutional Church, which implies some sort of infallibility in the acts of the ministry so that the consecration of the sacred species is effected by the prayer of the Church and absolution from sin by the pronouncement of the priest, the sacramental bond of marriage, *in foro Dei*, follows on the contract blessed by the Church as infallibly as the gift of an immortal soul on the physical generation of a human offspring. Yet, though the Church's ministry is so sublimely fruitful, it is neither an entirely sufficient nor an absolutely necessary condition for the gift of grace. It is not entirely sufficient, because it is not a question of a purely automatic effect of a physical kind. The sacraments always have, as it were, an element of uncertainty, which derives from the necessity for man to elicit an act of faith and commit himself to God for them to produce their effect. Nor is the intervention of the regular ministry an absolutely necessary condition for the imparting of grace. This point is so important and requires such close exposition that we will devote to it a special section.

* * *

(3) *The Spirit retains a certain freedom or autonomy which accounts for one of the features in the life of the Church*

What Scripture tells us is not confined to the propositions just stated concerning the bond of alliance between the Holy Spirit and the institutional Church. Though the activity of the Spirit is ever directed to the building up of the Church as the community of believers or of the saved, it is not presented as invariably bound up with the established means, but rather as preserving a kind of autonomy which shows itself in two series of facts—the charismata and the sudden visitations or unpredictable leadings of the Spirit.

The charismata appear in the New Testament as spiritual gifts of a manifest nature, which are ordered to the building up of the body of Christ and given directly by the Holy Spirit or the glorified Christ (Rom. xii; 1 Cor. xii. 4–11—the Spirit; xiv; Eph. iv. 11–12—the glorified Christ). Of course, there is no opposition between the charismata and the hierarchical ministry. In the first place, the ministers were themselves chosen from among those who had been given the gifts of the Spirit, and the Spirit too had intervened in their appointment (Acts xiii. 2–4; 1 Tim. iv. 14 to be compared with i. 18). Later we shall see to what extent the apostles and their fellow-workers were, so to speak, formed by the Holy Spirit. Likewise, it is clear, as Lightfoot showed in the chapter called *The Christian Ministry* in his commentary on the Philippians (1868), that many of the charismata enumerated by St. Paul represent actual ministries and strictly hierarchical functions. The ministers appointed in the early Church are seen to be essentially charismatic persons, filled with the Holy Ghost.[1] In this respect, the theology of the psuedo-Areopagite only systematized what was the ideal and, often enough, the actual case. In reality the charismata and the hierarchical functions overlap.

At the same time, long before the pastoral epistles and the so-called "catholicising" of Christianity supposed to have followed the death of the apostles, the charismatic inspiration was assimilated to the unity of the Church by being made subject to an objective rule of faith (1 Cor. xii. 13) and to the apostolic authority (1 Cor. xiv. 37–38). Just as the Holy Spirit has no radical autonomy, but is sent to do the work of Christ, to bring to mind what he said, the gifts imparted by the Spirit have no other end than to build up the body of Christ. Consequently, they have to be assimilated to the rule of apostolicity, which is that of continuity with the work done by the incarnate Word, under the double form of apostolicity of doctrine and apostolicity of ministry. These are, indeed, the two criteria of unity, and so of authenticity and validity, we have just met with in St. Paul.

[1] This is clear enough in the New Testament. Polycarp, bishop of Smyrna, is qualified as an "apostolic and prophetic teacher" (*Mart. Polyc.*, xvi. 2); the *Didache* (xv. 1) requires the election of bishops and deacons worthy of the Lord, men who are mild, disinterested, truthful and proven, "for they too fulfil, in your regard, the ministry of prophets and teachers".

If we read the epistle of Polycarp, bearing in mind the charismatic title given to him, we will be little likely to fall into the temptation of forming a romantic idea of the charismata and their possessors. The whole work has a classical and balanced quality.

We find them too in St. John (1 Jn. iv. 2, connected with iv. 6 and ii. 19). In both we find references to apostolicity of ministry and apostolicity of doctrine, the latter being, as it were, the internal content of the former, and, in addition, an insistence on submission by the faithful, however gifted spiritually they may seem to be, to the apostolicity of the ministry and, thereby, to the true apostolicity of doctrine. The spiritual gifts are assimilated to the unity of the Church through their regulation by the hierarchical ministry and the apostolic institution.

All the same, the charismata, a large number at any rate, do not arise from the hierarchical acts. But they are not unrelated to the hierarchical ministry and they have to be subject to it in order to be accepted in the Church for the building up of the body of Christ; still, they do not come from the apostolic ministry, but from the Spirit. We have here a whole body of facts of which the life of the Church has always been aware, which nothing in her theology gainsays, but which are practically ignored in present-day theology and ecclesiology. The facts, however, and the Scriptural texts are plain enough.

Invariably, the spiritual gifts present in the hierarchical organism of the ministry appear, at the same time, as having been freely given. This is especially the case with "prophecy", which occupies a very considerable place in the apostolic writings, from the Acts to the Apocalypse itself, notably in St. Paul. The early Church looked on itself as a Church in which the Spirit was continually raising up prophets and held this to be one of its most convincing features over against the Synagogue as well as the pagan world. The very same Church that claimed so close a bond between the acts of the hierarchy and the Holy Spirit (cf. Clement, Ignatius, Irenaeus, Cyprian) was conscious that it was built up, in addition, by additional supports given unexpectedly; its structure may be compared with that of a fabric made of a weft in conjunction with a warp. The apostles had previously shown hostility to a messianic work that did not proceed from their number (Mark iv. 37; Luke ix. 49–50); but, after Pentecost, they learned that, though the Spirit is the soul of the Church, he also breathes where he will. They realized that, if the imposition of their hands gave the Holy Spirit, he could come, too, before the apostolic sacrament (Acts x. 44–47) or through the imposition of other hands than theirs (ix. 17).

Finally, they found themselves confronted with a thirteenth apostle, an apostle through the direct intervention of the glorified Lord, one who credited himself with never having known Christ according to the flesh, an apostle by effraction, so to speak, yet one the Church does not hesitate to call, even to this day, purely and simply "the Apostle". It is true St. Paul made use of his authoritative status (1 Cor. iv. 21; v. 3, etc.), but he preferred to appeal to the spiritual gifts he had received and to the visible fruits of his apostolate (e.g. 1 Cor. vii. 40; 2 Cor. iii. 1–3; Gal. iv. 12, 20; 2 Cor. vii. 2). As an apostle added to the others over and above the normal rules of institution as such he seems to have preferred the criteria of life and effectiveness to those of structure and legitimacy. None the less, he was aware of the decisive importance of these. As the possessor of charismata would be unworthy of credit if he remained outside the institution and the apostolate set up by the will of God, Paul knew that he would be running in vain if he were not approved, both as to his teaching and his mission, by the apostolic centre at Jerusalem. It has been ably shown how solicitude for preserving unity and communion dominated St. Paul's conduct and is the real reason for his collection for the "Saints". We will go no further into these matters which are well known and, in any case, require to be treated on their own account. What concerns us here is the obvious duality of the ways in which the Spirit works, and so of those whereby he builds up the Church. They have been called, respectively, "Institution" and "Evenment", though they can hardly be fitted into a precise system. This duality is, admittedly, relative but it is real, none the less; what follows will make clearer the scope of each.

The Holy Spirit is continually at work to effect interiorly

what the hierarchical ministry does exteriorly, according to the bond of alliance between them that we have already explained. But he intervenes also directly and, in the first place, in the conduct of the apostles themselves, to direct, as it were, personally the growth of the Church and the building-up of the Mystical Body. Thus, there is not only the regular exercise of the powers or offices entrusted by Christ to his disciples, but together with, over and above, this, we might even say within it, a kind of sovereign liberty of action on the part of the Spirit, who is truly the "Lord of the apostolate". He effects all the increases in the Church (Acts ix. 31); he designates Paul and Barnabas for a mission to Cyprus (xiii. 2 and 4); he prevents Paul from going over to Asia (xvi. 6–7), but later, at any rate according to Codex D, he impels him to take the road to Macedonia (cf. Swete, *The Holy Spirit in the N.T.*, p. 105, n. 1). As regards St. Paul, his docility to the indications of the Spirit is conveyed by his repeated expression of a feeling that a door is opened to him in this or that place, or in the idea that, in the midst of dangers, the way remains open to him, which is a sign that he is still to bear fruit (Phil. i. 22). We find, too, in the other apostles—Peter in regard to Cornelius, Philip on the road to Gaza—the same docility to the sudden visitations and leadings of the Spirit. The particular personality of each of the apostles appears, in this way, as if moulded at every moment by the Holy Spirit who, the indwelling soul animating the Church, is also the ultimate ruler of the movements of the body. He inhabits and animates the institution, but the activity he unfolds within it is not reducible to the fact that he is given and bound closely to it. This activity of his makes it evident that, though given to the Church and faithful to the promises of the new alliance, he remains transcendent to the Church he dwells in; he is not just a divine force giving supernatural efficacy both to the ministry and to the sacraments, but a Person sovereignly active and free. He is not made use of by others, but himself directs events.

The episode of Philip and the eunuch of Candace is a striking example of how the Spirit acts by himself for the building up of the body of Christ. An interior inspiration urges Philip to take the road to Gaza and the statement of the Acts, that it was desert, seems to imply emphasis and, perhaps, motive. A strange inspiration, then; yet it is there that he meets the eunuch in his chariot, a meeting like so many that chance puts in our way as time goes on. But the inspiration becomes more detailed; on seeing this man unknown to him, met by chance, Philip feels impelled to speak to him. The rest is familiar enough: how the meeting gives occasion to Philip to tell the man about Christ, and concludes with the celebration, by baptism, of the mystery of water and the Spirit.

This kind of thing, which seems so extraordinary to some, has always occurred and still does. The body of Christ is built up by the regular mediation, functional and hierarchical, of the appointed ministers, the sacraments and the other rites of the Church, but also by the unpredictable, occasional and fraternal mediation of the various conjunctures and unexpected happenings brought about by the Spirit and signs of his working, which he offers to souls ready to accept them. A whole volume could be filled with examples drawn from the lives of saints and men of God, from one's own experience and that of many others who have confided in us. The *Confessions* of St. Augustine, for instance, contain many examples of what may be called the law of occasions or conjunctures: Alypius attending, by chance, a lecture given by Augustine when still a Manichean and, by what he heard, delivered from his passion for the theatre and the circus; Augustine himself hearing Pontianus tell about the life of St. Anthony and being fired with spiritual ambition in company with Alypius (*Surgunt indocti . . .*), and shortly after, in the garden, hearing, as if sung over and over again by some child, the *tolle, lege* and then chancing on the epistles of St. Paul. How often, too, in the history of the Church, important decisions about vocations, foundations, even canons of Councils, have been taken as a result of a dream, a word, a consultation of Scripture, in short of an intervention of the type of "evenment"; and this, not only in the first and second centuries, which abound in such cases, but during the whole of the Middle Ages and, doubtless, later as well. This subject, which has never been studied as a whole, certainly deserves investigation. We ourselves are convinced, as a result of a few haphazard soundings, that there could be disclosed here one of the most constant and decisive elements in the Church's life.

Thus we are led by various ways to admit that, if the Church is always the work of the Holy Spirit who dwells in it, it is not that of the Spirit exclusively as bound to the institution and working in and through it. The Holy Spirit retains a kind of freedom of action which is immediate, autonomous and personal. In this way, there exists a kind of free sector which constitutes one of the most salient features of the life of the Church.

Is it possible, after having established this fact, to give an explanation of it in terms of causality?

Of the four causes involved in every question of causality, the material cause is here beyond doubt; as regards the Church, it is mankind. Nor have we to discuss the final cause, for it is one and the same for all the agencies at work for the fulfilment of the plan of God's grace. Consequently, it is to the efficient and formal causes that we must look for an explanation of the facts brought to light in the preceding pages. It will be readily understood that this is no place to undertake a detailed explanation of the Church's theology of efficient and formal causes, which would require a special treatise. All we shall do is to summarize, in schematic form, the general position. One of the most interesting points to be elucidated is the articulation of the formal to the efficient cause. In a society such as the Church, the realizing cause, which is the instituting authority, becomes the formal principle by entering into the group and forming part of it as its organizing authority. That is why the apostles, the builders of the Church which is the temple of God (1 Cor. iii. 9–17), are also spoken of as its foundation (Eph. ii. 20); from being the initiators of the work from outside it they become its formal and organizing element.

EFFICIENT CAUSE (bringing into existence)—CHRIST, as sending

The apostolic body	The Holy Spirit
↓	↓

both of these, as realizing the Church, are efficient causes, but in the Church once realized, become

Formal Cause (indwelling and composing)	Quasi-formal Cause (soul indwelling, but not composing)

FORMAL CAUSE:

Static	Dynamic	
		↓
= form of order		
= the *gradus et ordines* of the Church, which assign and qualify the members; but chiefly the hierarchical degrees, that is, the Authority, the powers of the Institution.	= form of action realising the common good	distributing the functions and giving to the powers, sacraments, etc., their efficacity, by reason of the bond of alliance already spoken of.
		↓
	= active orientation towards unity *in Christ* governed externally by the apostolic Authority — and internally by	the Holy Spirit
		↓
	orientation of all the spiritual gifts: sanctifying grace, the theological and moral virtues, gifts of the Holy Spirit, gifts of all kinds, especially the charismata, given	distributing gifts *prout vult* (1 Cor. xii. 11), and making them concur.
(*Order of structure*)		↓

Ad utilitatem, ad aedificationem corporis Christi.

(*Order of life*)

Other points, too, call for explanation, such as the ideas of static form (organization) and dynamic form (common action, co-operation for a common end), that of quasi-formal cause, etc. As it is, we make no claim to comprise the whole theology of the Church in this scheme; it is simply intended to clarify the questions under discussion. The scheme is on page 181.

The institutional Church, the Church in its outward structure, is wholly dependent on, and continuous with, the Incarnate Word and the messianic energies in which the apostolic powers share. The Holy Spirit, the Spirit of the Son, sent by him and proceeding from him, gives force and efficacy to these powers both when exercised in proclaiming the faith and in celebrating the sacraments of faith, as is affirmed in countless passages of Scripture. As we have seen, this results from the bond of alliance existing between the Church and the Holy Spirit.

In the sphere of the Church's life, the Holy Spirit is at work once again as sent by the Son to accomplish his work. But here it is no longer just a question of simply making effective the powers instituted by Christ, of the effective realization of a structure laid down by the incarnate Word in his life on earth; it is a question of the realization of a work being actively pursued by the glorified Christ, the head in heaven of the body he builds up for himself on earth. The Lord remains himself transcendent to his body. Certainly, his promise remains embedded in the institutional Church; its essential, structural features are fixed for all time and can be clearly seen. The Church's weft, to recur to the image suggested above, holds no surprises; but its warp, consisting of the exercise of all the gifts imparted to individuals, derives from the free movement of the grace which Christ from heaven distributes in accordance with a plan fixed and known by him alone. The unpredictable character of all we have spoken of under the headings of charismata, divine interventions, conjunctures and occasions, bears witness to the transcendence of the head in regard to the body—without prejudice, assuredly, to the consequences of man's freedom to accept or refuse, to allow the seed of grace to bear fruit or to leave it to weaken and wither.

It is not, however, sufficient to adduce as an explanation the transcendence the Head keeps in regard to the body. Many passages, as we know, speak, in this connection, not so much of (the heavenly) Christ, as of the Holy Spirit—in particular, 1 Cor. ii. 4–11, where the Spirit is spoken of as, indeed, a person and not simply as a force. Various texts of the Acts we have already met with have the same tenor. Consequently, the freedom shown in the gifts and initiatives by which the body of Christ is built up as regards what we have called the warp is not indicative solely of the transcendence of the Head; it derives equally from the fact that the Church proceeds from a duality of missions and divine Persons. No doubt, the Holy Spirit is the Spirit of Jesus and accomplishes no other work than that of Christ; it is also true that the perfect unity and simplicity of God, the perfect consubstantiality of the divine Persons, involve a common will of the Spirit, the Son and the Father, Yet Scripture attributes to each of them acts as if proper to each; and we cannot go wrong if we use the same language. As the innermost mystery of the Three Persons is revealed in Scripture from their function in the economy of salvation, it is easily understandable that interventions which bear the stamp of freedom and personality should make it manifest that the Church is the work of Christ and of the Holy Spirit, the fruit of two distinct personal missions.

In the life of the Church, as in our individual lives, the Holy Spirit, the active principle of all in the supernatural order, is so interior to the creature that his action is virtually indistinguishable from that of the creature in question. Thus St. Paul speaks indifferently of the Spirit of adoption by which we cry: Abba, Father, and of the Spirit as himself uttering in us the filial cry of our hearts.[1] Every Christian knows that whatever is good in him

[1] Rom. viii. 15 and Gal. iv. 6. Cf. Rom. ix. 1 and viii. 16. We owe this idea to Swete, *The Holy Catholic Church*, London, 1915, pp. 111–115.

comes from the Holy Spirit, and the Church knows and confesses that this same Spirit gives existence and efficaciousness to whatever of value she does in furtherance of the kingdom of God. Still, it is good, as well in the Church as in our own lives, that God (the Holy Spirit), by acting directly, alone, in unpredictable and sovereign fashion, gives, from time to time, positive testimony that he alone is the Lord and author of life, *Dominum et vivificantem.*

All that has been said above enables us to gain a better understanding of the difference between an ecclesiology of life and an ecclesiology of structure or, we might equally well say, between a pneumatological and a christological ecclesiology. In this regard, Möhler's theological development is highly instructive. In his early lectures on Canon Law he followed the general ideas of the theological schools, but later reacted against their way of presenting the Church, which was, in fact, not only that of eighteenth century scholosticism, but was to be found, too, in the *Kirchenrecht* of F. Walter, the *Kirchengeschichte* of Katerkamp, and in J. de Maistre's *Du Pape*. He objected to this kind of ecclesiology on the ground of its naturalism. It conceived the Church in the same way as any secular organization, so that it all seemed to consist in the juridical order of the hierarchy and this order, once established, was quite sufficient, so that there was no call to speak of a continuously vivifying action on the part of God—"God created the hierarchy, and so provided more than adequately for the needs of the Church right to the end of the world". This was how Möhler summarized the attitude of an ecclesiology which had its source in the Counter-reformation and the Enlightenment and which is still, it must be admitted, that of many catechisms and expositors of our own time.

In contrast with this, Möhler wished to expound a Church which was pneumatic and charismatic. In the first flush of his reaction, in 1823, he grossly underestimated the importance of the hierarchical function. Even in the *Unity in the Church* (1825), where the hierarchical principle finds a place in the general scheme,

Möhler continued to set out an ecclesiology frankly centred on the Holy Spirit, as he himself acknowledged in the preface. The Church of the *Unity* is not built up from outside and above, but from the interior, from the Spirit of love who, by bringing the faithful to unity, seeks to "corporify himself"[1]; the decisive element is the interior spirit, the source whence proceeds external unity, by a movement going from within to without. The institutional side of the Church has, in regard to this spirit, not so much a causal function as a function of expression, admittedly necessary and willed by God. Möhler gives it a place, but an inadequate one and, on that score, has been justly criticized in the name of Catholic tradition and reality.

Moreover, he corrected himself in his later works, *Athanasius the Great*, the *Symbolism*, which he amended more and more in successive editions, and the *Defence of the Symbolik*. But what is most significant is that, in correcting his earlier ideas, he was obliged to construct his ecclesiology from a definitely Christological standpoint. The comparison with Protestantism made Möhler realize the value, not merely of expression, but of causality and structure belonging to the visible institution in regard to the spirit and to communion in faith and love. The *Symbolism* does not overlook union in love, but links it to the incarnational principle and to the necessity of an outward *means*.

The present task of ecclesiology, helped on, as it is in these days, by so much valuable work that has been done on the subject, by the teachings of the Magisterium and by so much activity in the spiritual and apostolic spheres, is to maintain both poles whose co-ordinates we have sought to trace, even though a certain tension between them is bound to remain. The encyclical *Mystici Corporis* of June 1943 teaches that the Church is, at one and the same time, a Church of law and a Church of love; that it is constituted by a double mission, a juridical one which is the basis of the apostolic powers as a continuation of Christ's messianic

1 "The entire constitution of the Church is nothing else than love corporified": *Unity*, para. 64, at the beginning.

action, and a spiritual and vivifying one which is none other than that of the Holy Spirit; that the Church was born at Pentecost, since it as then sent and proclaimed to the world, but that its institution is linked up with the cross of Christ and even to the different moments of the ministry he fulfilled while on earth; and finally that it is a living body, the body of Christ, not only by reason of its being a communion of all who live by the Spirit of Christ, but as a body ordered by Christ through its ministries and the visible sacraments deriving from his Incarnation. The various texts, facts and arguments used in the present study fall quite naturally into the framework of this teaching. They may be summed up as follows:

There is a duality of agents (or of missions) that realize the work of Christ, the Spirit working internally, with a divine efficaciousness, what the apostolic ministry effects externally, he himself, to that end, being bound by a bond of alliance, in virtue of God's fidelity to his promises.

The Church owes its structure to the institution of the means of grace, deriving from the *acta Christi in carne*. It is fundamentally Christological.

But it lives, under the government of the glorified Christ, by the action of the Holy Spirit. Its life is thus a sphere in which the transcendence of its Head and the personality, equally transcendent, of the Spirit are manifested in the sovereign liberty of their gifts and interventions.